# $ELLING *on the* NET

## THE COMPLETE GUIDE

DATE DUE

# $ELLING *on the* NET

## THE COMPLETE GUIDE

# HERSCHELL GORDON LEWIS
# ROBERT D. LEWIS

*Printed on recyclable paper*

**NTC Business Books**
a division of *NTC Publishing Group* • Lincolnwood, Illinois USA

**Library of Congress Cataloging-in-Publication Data**

Lewis, Herschell Gordon, 1926-
    Selling on the net : the complete guide / by Herschell Gordon
Lewis, Robert D. Lewis, 1952-
      p.  cm.
    Includes index.
    ISBN 0-8442-3233-5 (alk. paper). — ISBN 0-8442-3234-3 (pbk. :
alk. paper)
    1. Internet marketing.  2. Internet advertising.  I. Lewis,
Robert D., 1952–  . II. Title.
    HF5415.1265.L483   1996
    658.8'00285'467—dc20                 96-23087
                                           CIP

Published by NTC Business Books, a division of NTC Publishing Group
4255 West Touhy Avenue
Lincolnwood (Chicago), Illinois 60646–1975, U.S.A.

6 7 8 9 RM 9 8 7 6 5 4 3 2 1

# Contents

# Preface

## What This Book Isn't . . . And What It Is

If you're looking for a book loaded with technical terms, arcane programming procedures, and electronic in-talk, except for Chapter One this isn't it.

Yes, we've included some technobabble in Chapter One. That's because the creative process—the subject of this book—has to lean on the technical process, bringing up the images the way they're supposed to come up. The procedure parallels the copywriter depending on a production artist for font selection and arrangement of images. If that copywriter is totally illiterate (or contemptuous) relative to the graphics, he or she deserves to have the message crash.

But once we're past the procedural descriptions, this book is about a subject right out of a science-fiction story.

No, it's not a monster, but, like some sci-fi monsters, it seems to double in size every day. It develops new facets every day. It makes instant bums out of self-declared heroes. It spawns terminology that—more like Dr. Jekyll and Mr. Hyde than an expanding universe—not only changes every day but has its own totality of lexicographical goobledygook, assuring today's Web-literate expert that tomorrow he or she will have a case of Egg-On-Face Disease, curable only by a frantic search through that day's newly published list of Internet terminology.

The major problem faced by anyone who wants to codify rules for Internet marketing is the suddenness of the medium. Television grew quickly during the late 1940s and early 1950s, but that growth was positively leisurely compared with the Internet. In the year 1993 almost no one even knew what it was. By the year 1996 individual sites, among the hundreds of thousands already in existence, were measuring "hits" in the hundreds of millions, and marketers were leaping into the medium not because of sound business decisions but because "everybody else is there."

The illustrations in this book aren't intended to be "high resolution." They're just as you'd see them on the Web, except that they aren't reproduced in color. And please understand: your computer screen is horizontal, and pages are vertical. To experience a page properly, your computer is the only answer.

We have discovered (by exploring other books on the subject) that positioning this book is easier than we first had thought. *Marketing* is, to us, the application of salesmanship to a specific circumstance. That's what this book is about.

So if your interest is applying salesmanship to the Web, come in and browse. You'll find both principles and examples of those principles. Probably you'll unearth some prejudices, too. But the prejudices are aimed at (in our opinion) ineffective, arrogant, and over-arty misuse of the medium.

Welcome to this new, fascinating, and absolutely incredible electronic jungle!

Herschell Gordon Lewis
Robert D. Lewis

# Acknowledgments

We're indebted to Richard Hagle and the editorial staff of NTC Business Books for assigning this project to us. And to others named Lewis—Margo, Ruth, Kimberly, and Erin—our thanks for encouragement and tolerance.

The Direct Marketing Association, which scheduled several creative seminars on this subject, forced us into logical and coherent organization of subject matter. The magazines *Direct Marketing* and *InfoWorld,* for which the authors write regular columns, provided an early forum for some of the concepts you will see in these pages.

And to Tim Berners-Lee—the almost unknown genius who literally invented the World Wide Web—we, and everyone associated with this soon-to-be-gigantic enterprise owe eternal gratitude.

# **1** What Is the Internet, Anyway?

In his nifty science-fiction novel *Neuromancer*, William Gibson coined the term *cyberspace*. The term promptly caught on, to the extreme annoyance of computer scientists and network vendors who wanted to assign a dry, forgettable acronym to the same concept, but hadn't yet gotten around to it.

The term lacks a concise definition, but here's a good (borrowed) way of understanding what it is. When Alexander Graham Bell invented the telephone, cyberspace sprang into existence as the place where telephone conversations take place. When only the telephone allowed two-way (or with conference calls, many-way) conversations, cyberspace lacked much interest or dimension.

# The Increased Interest in the Internet

Technology has made cyberspace more interesting in the past several years. People who "live" in it exchange printed information in real-time (they "chat"); they send electronic mail through it; they also exchange or broadcast drawings, photographs, sound clips, and even movies. (Somebody even invented a way to transmit smells, but like the "smellovision" of old, it never caught on. Thank goodness.)

Often, thinking about the Internet in terms of cyberspace—a place, with its own laws, conventions, and ecology—can help you think through issues that would otherwise remain murky.

Terms like the *Internet, World Wide Web, virtual reality, cyberspace, the Information Superhighway (or I-way or Infobahn),* have captured the imagination of the American public over the past several years. Since you're holding this book in your hands, you presumably have encountered these terms and have a passing interest and at least a vague notion that there's something out there you should know more about.

Most people in business have a lot in common with the '49ers (of the California Gold Rush). Somewhere west of here, *California* has gold in its hills. If you can only find the motherlode, you'll be *rich!*

The current round of Internet fever is the Gold Rush of the 1990s. Some people—those who, along with their dreams, have prepared well, educated themselves about the discipline, planned well and thoroughly, and left their illusions behind—*will* strike gold and get rich. A second group will, like Levi Strauss, make a lot of money selling one kind of provision or another to the prospectors. The third group will spend a lot of time and effort and have little to show for it.

This book will help you join the first group and stay out of the third.

# Beginning at the Beginning

Let's start with the basics: what, ignoring the hype, are the Internet, Cyberspace, Information Superhighway and the rest?

*Internet* is short for *Internetwork*. You can think of the Internet as a shared facility for linking networks of computers together into one giant supernetwork.

Here's what makes the Internet amazing: nobody's in charge. In violation of most management and computer theory, it's an anarchic concoction in which, so long as you agree to abide by some basic rules, you can do pretty much whatever you want.

In this way, somewhere between fifty thousand and fifty million computers interconnect without any central control or organizing scheme, somehow exchanging electronic mail, computer programs, electronic documents, and an uncataloged assortment of other kinds of information.

And it keeps on expanding. According to two different estimates, it will have either 200 million or a billion users by the end of the year 2000. One consequence of the Internet's uncontrolled existence is that nobody knows how big it really is.

The Internet, by modern standards, uses seriously outmoded technology held together by ingenious electronic patches, improvisations, chewing gum and Band-Aids, with the occasional bent paperclip thrown in when nothing else will do. It began as a research project called ARPANET (Advanced Research Projects Association Network) funded by the federal government as a way to link research institutions' computers. It quickly evolved into a network connecting most major research institutions in the country, primarily colleges and universities.

Academics don't think like the business community or the military. The Internet became a worldwide entity early in its existence, and by now it would be nearly impossible to create anything like national borders with passports, visas, and checkpoints.

Academics don't think in terms of security very much, so the Internet wasn't built to foil burglars, vandals, or spies. The academics built it to help them share information—security systems have the opposite purpose—and so the only security built into the Internet is there to keep it running. (Computers linked to the Internet may have elaborate security measures; the Internet itself has very little.)

The builders of the Internet mostly used an operating system called UNIX, invented in Bell Labs as a research project. Bell Labs gave away copies of the UNIX program to anyone who wanted them, and a generation of computer science students enhanced it, added to it, and modified it through a series of Ph.D. theses, class projects, and practical jokes. In Darwinian fashion, those that filled some useful niche survived and propagated.

That's the kind of attitude that built the Internet. It's something like a frontier town with a unique sense of community but no real organization or zoning laws.

The Internet does have a very important characteristic of a physical community: everyone on the Internet has an address. Actually, they have two. The first is a physical address specified by the "Internet Protocol" (The "IP Address"), which consists of a 32-bit hexadecimal number (don't worry about it), and which means the Internet can have 4,294,967,296 different addresses (minus a couple of numbers that have been reserved for house-keeping purposes). Think of the IP Address as your longitude and latitude. You know you have one, but that doesn't mean you want to know what it is.

Your second Internet address is your "domain name." That's the one *you* use. Domain names have two parts: an organizational name and its type. For example, the ever-popular ABC Corporation might have a domain name of *abc.com*. A group called the InterNIC assigns domain names on a first-come first-served basis, and charges (currently) the stiff fee of $50 per year for them. Organizations come in several types: *.com* for commercial organizations, *.org* for nonprofit organizations, *.edu* for educational institutions, *.gov* for governmental agencies, *.net* for network providers, along with one each for every foreign country (the Internet may be an international entity, but it's headquartered in the United States).

Many people think the term *Information Superhighway* refers to the Internet, but it doesn't. Vice President Gore coined the term to describe something he wants to build to replace the Internet. Since it doesn't exist, it has wondrous properties: near-infinite capacity to deliver information, complete security to support financial transactions, dirt-cheap operation so nobody will be left out, and. . . .

The Internet has one huge technological advantage over the Information Superhighway (also called the I-way and Infobahn). It exists. It works. You can do real useful things on it right now. So far, its academic masters have been able to adapt it to an extraordinarily wide range of uses.

Before getting to any of them, a few more words on cyberspace.

# The Cyberspace Community

Have you ever been to a social gathering at which somebody (let's pick on insurance salesmen) walks in and starts trying to sell insurance to everyone in sight?

"What a boor," you think as you try to avoid the embarrassing creature.

If you build the habit of thinking of cyberspace as a *place* which has communities of inhabitants who moved in long before you did (think New England) and which has evolved a unique culture, mores, and code of ethics, then you can avoid many of the pitfalls that befall marketing-oriented business professionals who first encounter the Internet.

Like a boorish salesman at any other social gathering, a boorish salesman in cyberspace will alienate potential customers instead of attracting them.

The term used on the Internet to describe its social conventions is *netiquette*.

You can find some elaborate writings describing the rules of netiquette. The best way to learn it, though, is to spend some time in cyberspace observing the interactions of long-time inhabitants.

To avoid offending your best prospects, think in terms of working in a small town which hasn't bothered to enact strong zoning laws because it expects its citizens to behave responsibly. Cyberspace operates under such a libertarian political philosophy.

While the Internet lacks formal zoning laws, its denizens have, by consensus, zoned some areas for various forms of commerce, while others have a more . . . residential . . . flavor.

The citizens of cyberspace understand commerce and consumerism, but generally don't approve of hard-core selling, except in the area known as the *World Wide Web*.

Just as you might invite an insurance salesman into your home while hanging up on a telemarketer who calls you during dinner, so cybercitizens might accept product information through the Internet from someone they know while otherwise complaining bitterly about unscrupulous marketers on the Net.

Of all the uses of the Internet, marketers have focused most of their attention on the World Wide Web. And for good reason: it's intensely graphical, far easier for novice technologists to reach and navigate, and far more similar to better-known media than the rest of the services available on the Internet. In fact, most of this book deals with selling on the World Wide Web.

Savvy marketers will make use of other parts of the Internet as well, while carefully abiding by the rules of netiquette. And so, before describing the World Wide Web, here are a few other Internet services, along with some suggestions on how you can best take advantage of them.

## ELECTRONIC MAIL

The granddaddy of all Internet applications, and the most widely used, electronic mail (e-mail) lets you cheaply and easily send information to correspondents all over the globe.

You send e-mail to the Internet address of your intended recipient. If you wanted to send a message to Joan Smith at ABC Incorporated, you might address it to *Joan.Smith@abc.com*, assuming ABC Inc. assigned addresses in that format. Joan Smith might also be called *JSmith@abc.com; JoanS@abc.com;* or *Joan Smith@abc.com;* or whatever else the network weenies at ABC Inc. decided. How do you know? Look at her business card. If she's smart, she put her address on it.

Internet addresses don't always provide a clue to your correspondent's identity. If someone has a private Internet account through a local Internet Access Provider, he could easily call himself *shirley.temple@iap.net* and you'd never know he didn't have a cute face and curly red hair.

Two niceties. First, you pronounce @ as "at" and the period as "dot" so you pronounce *JSmith@abc.com* as "JSmith at abc dot com." Second, a lot of hard-core Internet wonks emulate e. e. cummings, and use only lower case.

Here's an easy way to infer the resume of a correspondent who comes from the world of technology: programmers who cut their teeth in the mainframe world will often type their whole message in upper-case letters, BECAUSE MAINFRAME GUYS DON'T UNDERSTAND WHAT PURPOSE THOSE PESKY LOWER-CASE LETTERS SERVE ANYWAY. Programmers who come out of the world of UNIX, as mentioned, only use lower-case letters in their messages, because, john, you and i know that pressing the shift key takes too much effort.

Those of us who started out with typewriters and graduated to personal computers generally type normally.

**Using E-mail.** You can't do much in the way of formatting electronic mail. You can't even underline text unless you and your correspondent use the same word processor . . . but Internet junkies have invented several (admittedly hokey :-) ) conventions to get around the limitations of straight text. For example the symbol ":-)" when viewed sideways, turns into a smiley-face: an example of what are known as "emoticons." Here's another —";-)"—I'm winking at you. =|(:-)> is Abe Lincoln, complete with stovepipe hat and beard. And so on.

You'll also find parenthetical explanations of intent, most

commonly "(grin)" which let's you know the writer was just kidding. Some writers also embed a word in asterisks to let you know they want it *emphasized*.

What does e-mail have to do with selling on the Internet? Plenty, so long as you're smart and polite.

First and most basic: since more than 60 percent of all business employees and more than 80 percent of all government employees use e-mail, you can use it as an exceptionally convenient medium for cementing relationships. Your customers will send you e-mail when they'd never bother sending you its paper-based equivalent (*snail-mail* in the Internaut's jargon).

Why? If you're asking, you've never used e-mail. You don't have to wait at a printer, you don't need to fold the letter, you don't need to address an envelope, affix a stamp, or take the letter to the mailbox. With e-mail you write it, address it, and twang the magic twanger.

People in the United States today feel powerless, which explains why they don't vote and feel generally grumpy during an economic expansion of extraordinary duration. E-mail empowers them. Exploit that feeling. Encourage its use by your customers to tell you what they're thinking. *Return their messages with messages of your own, so they know they've been heard.* Even if you have to set up a software "robot" to send a basic acknowledgment, you'll have added a bit of additional strength to your relationship with that customer.

Here's another wonderful use of e-mail: set up a list server. List servers let Infonauts automatically subscribe to electronic publications. They do so by sending a specially coded message to a specific e-mail address. A simple program extracts the sender's e-mail address and adds it to a distribution list.

Set up a list server and use it to deliver your monthly newsletter to customers and prospects. You get two big benefits from exceptionally cheap technology:

1.  You've taken another step in cementing relationships with your customers.

2.  You get a free list of qualified leads. And, yes, *everyone* who voluntarily adds his or her name to your subscription list is fair game for your marketing efforts.

Just make sure of the following:

1.  *Don't* care at all if the messages you send via e-mail get passed along to an unpredictable number of additional recipients.

2.  *Do* include instructions on how to subscribe and cancel subscriptions at the bottom of every newsletter (so that people who get a free copy from a friend know where it came from, and how to get a copy directly from you instead).

3.  *Do* also include information on how to contact a real, live, human being by e-mail at the bottom of each newsletter. This is a lot like making sure people can always reach an operator from your voice mail system by pressing zero.

4.  *Do* send something people will want to see—or they'll quickly *un*subscribe.

Once they give you their e-mail address, they're fair game for additional correspondence so long as you don't get carried away and overdo it. On the other hand, don't send unsolicited marketing letters to a distribution list you've gathered up from some external source. This violates netiquette. If you're not sure they want the information, don't send it.

The Internet community frowns on electronic junk mail, and for good reason: unlike snail mail, the recipient pays to receive mail on the Internet.

A last note on e-mail: the ease with which you can quickly exchange messages creates a hazard—the dreaded "flame" (scathing message). With snail mail, you have a chance to reconsider as you print your scathing diatribe, address an envelope, fold the letter, put it in the envelope, seal the envelope, apply a stamp, and walk it over to a mailbox. With e-mail, you point, click, and offend your closest friend.

More to the point, you'll inevitably receive flames from customers. Don't worry too much about it. You're getting useful informations about shortcomings in your service. Ignore the intonation and pay attention to the meaning behind it.

# USENET

While electronic mail provides the greatest immediate benefit on the Internet, and the World Wide Web provides the most sizzle, in Usenet you'll find the heart of the Internet's unique culture.

*Usenet* is the name given to the technology used for interactive discussion groups, also called News Groups. People participate in News Groups by reading "postings" and adding their own.

News Groups come in two flavors: refereed and unrefereed. The former have something in common with scientific journals in that somebody takes responsibility for screening the postings that go into them. The latter can range from genteel discsussions about fashion to rough-and-tumble disagreements (flame wars) about the social value of pornography that have more in common with a barroom brawl than you'd expect in a high-tech medium.

You can find discussion groups on Usenet on every imaginable, and many unimaginable, subjects: cats, black holes, existentialism, psoriasis, obsessive-compulsive disorder, vile and disgusting habits . . . even computers. If you're faint of heart, don't browse through Usenet, especially the discussion "threads" that begin with alt. These discussions range from the profound to banal to scatological, and many participants lack any pretense of inhibition.

Usenet can be fun. When you hear about people spending far too many hours on the Internet, chances are you're hearing about Usenet junkies.

Here's some good advice: participate in Usenet as a hobby first. Don't even think about using it for marketing purposes until you're well-established and have learned its style and culture. When you get the hang of it, you may find opportunities to quietly offer help, just as an attorney might say to a friend, "Stop by the office next week and we'll look at that." Much beyond that and you'll find yourself a pariah.

And believe it: You don't want the Internet community annoyed with you if you plan to use the Internet as a marketing medium. They know more than you do and have an arsenal of weapons at their disposal to wreak havoc on your Internet activities if they choose to.

You don't believe it? Here's just one example: the "PING bomb." PING is one of those acronyms whose actual meaning doesn't matter. Its name explains its function. When you PING a device on the Internet, you send out a single packet. The Internet break messages into discrete chunks, called "frames" or "packets," which the receiver has to reassemble into useful information.

That packet has only one function: to elicit a response packet so you can verify that you can send and receive other packets later on. If a bunch of Internauts get mad at you, they can program some of their old, spare computers to continually PING your system, which won't be able to do anything on the Internet other than acknowledge the PINGs all day long. And that's a fairly innocuous form of revenge as these things go.

## FTP

FTP stands for *File Transfer Protocol*. Long before the World Wide Web, many institutions set up FTP sites as repositories for useful information, available for downloading to authorized individuals. (Some institutions set up "anonymous FTP" servers accessible to anyone—no authorization necessary.)

Until the advent of the World Wide Web, only the technically adept (or at least the technically brave) took advantage of FTP sites. While a treasure trove of computer programs and informative documents awaits those visitors who brave the

Internet to find them, so do a wide a variety of complex, time-consuming file compression techniques. Worse, you never know when the program you download contains a computer virus just waiting to give your computer the cyberflu.

One other bit of technobabble you'll need to understand to properly appreciate the potential of an FTP site: the Internet community has largely converged on a document-formatting standard from Adobe Systems called the "Portable Document Format" or PDF. You can take any formatted document, such as you'd create with your word processor or desktop publishing program, and store it as a PDF file. Anybody with the Adobe Acrobat viewer program will see pretty much the same thing you saw when you created the document.

With the advent of the World Wide Web, FTP sites have gained a new dimension because you can use the Web as a friendlier way to provide access to an FTP site. That means you can make technical manuals, position papers, press releases, books, magazines—anything you want to give away, including free software if you choose to do so—available through your Web site.

## THE WORLD WIDE WEB

The World Wide Web, or the Web, as everyone calls it, has generated as much excitement as Windows/95, and without Bill Gates's PR machine and promotion budget. Originally invented by Tim Berners-Lee, a software designer at the European nuclear physics laboratory CERN, it has captured the imagination of millions as few developments ever have.

But what exactly *is* the Web (and do you care)?

Take a few minutes to learn the basics about the Web. You need to know some of the technical details because they'll help you understand some of the Web's oddest characteristics, and because they'll help you come up with new and innovative uses for it, instead of trying to make it do things it's mostly incapable of.

## Warning! Technical stuff follows! Brace yourself!

While you wouldn't know it from all the hoopla, the entire World Wide Web consists of a naming convention (a standard way of identifying the location of a document), a fairly simple scheme for embedding codes inside text, and a file transfer "protocol." (You'll see the word *protocol* a lot in discussions of the Internet. It means an agreed-on, standard way for two machines to communicate.)

The naming convention defines the "Universal Resource Locator" or URL, which is the address of a Web home page. URLs always begin *http://* and usually take the form *http://www.domain-name* so that our old friend ABC Incorporated would use *http://www.abc.com*. That's the URL of the so-called "home page," which will be the first document anyone sees on your Web site. Other pages generally have names of varying levels of complexity that follow the domain-name, such as *http://www.abc.com/directory/subdirectory/veryimportant.doc*. Some companies on the Web provide directories to the rest of the Web. Because of the way Web browsers work, nobody has to pay any attention at all to anything beyond your URL. Any company doing business on the World Wide Web should register its URL with every directory it can find. Yahoo! is one of the better-known on-line directories. It acts as both a table of contents and searchable index. Others are WebCrawler, Lycos, Excite, and Alta Vision.

HTML, the scheme for embedding codes, stands for "HyperText Markup Language." Hypertext means you can embed a "link" from one document to another. In a sense, it's a very fancy bibliographic reference. Instead of just mentioning another document, you create a link to it, so that a reader just has to point to the reference with a mouse, click, and go directly to that document.

In the terminology of text processing, a markup code is simply a code you'd embed in a stream of text to control how that text ought to be handled, a concept left over from the days when you couldn't simply click on an icon to make a bunch of text italicized.

HTML codes differ from the kinds of formatting concepts

you've become accustomed to through personal computer word processors. Most of the codes don't specify formatting information. Instead, what they describe is one step removed from the actual format. They describe the document part (Heading, Title) or a degree of emphasis (Strong) as well as providing specific formatting information (Center).

Instructions on how to translate each of these document parts or other descriptions into specific formatting information reside in the browser software. This means the reader, not the author, has final control over the actual format of the document.

You may find this loss of format and layout control horrifying, but it provides several advantages. First, distinguishing between the purpose of a bunch of text and its appearance on a computer screen makes the process of improving HTML much easier—just add another code to the official lexicon and you're done. Browsers generally ignore any code they don't recognize, so the document will remain readable by all generations of Web browsers.

Second, accommodating the physically impaired becomes a much easier task. Those with weak eyesight can use bigger fonts. Text-to-speech readers can (in principle—nobody does this yet) use different intonations to reflect different document parts or text contexts.

Last and most important, the creator of a document doesn't have to plan on a particular display technology. Different personal computer displays have different dimensions and resolutions. Laser printers print in "portrait" mode—vertically—and they don't print in color, while computers display in landscape mode—horizontally—in full color. Color inkjet printers also print in portrait mode, and so on. And best of all, personal computers running Windows, others running OS/2, Macintoshes, UNIX systems, and even old-fashioned "dumb terminals" can interpret HTML codes into formatting that works within each of their strengths and limitations.

And then there's the Web's File Transfer Protocol. Here's the short version: when you enter a URL into your Web browser, the browser sends a message to something called a "Domain Name

Server," which tells it the IP Address that corresponds to that URL. Your browser then sends a message to that IP Address asking the corresponding Web server to send a copy of the file containing the home page document to you using the Hypertext Transfer Protocol (HTTP, remember?). When your browser gets the home page, it renders it on your computer screen using a stored set of rules to translate the HTML codes embedded in the document into a readable screen format.

Finally, when you click on a hypertext link (usually an icon in the document or text that's underlined and displayed in a different color), your browser sends a message back to the Web server asking for the address of whatever document corresponds to that link. On receiving the address it then repeats the previous process but for the linked document. And so forth.

End of Technical Stuff! Congratulations on making it through.

You should find knowledge of how it all actually works helpful in planning your Web site.

But not too helpful: Knowing the workings of the internal combustion engine, automatic transmission, rack-and-pinion steering, and disk brake mechanism gives you only limited knowledge of how to drive a car.

And so . . .

## Beginning of strained Cyberspace metaphor describing the Web

Think of the Web as the Mall of America of Cyberspace. It's the commercial district. It's the place where rambunctious architecture, graffiti, endless rows of billboards, shops, restaurants, and department stores all vie for the attention of casual strollers who really just want either entertainment or information, or, best of all, "edutainment," which gives them useful information in an enjoyable, entertaining form.

This mall differs from real malls in that real malls have space outside the stores where shoppers stroll, looking at storefronts. In the Web, shoppers always have to be inside someplace or other, often for just long enough to decide they'd rather be some-where else.

Some shops have doors into other shops—you can easily put in a hypertext link to someone else's Web site—and some shops do nothing except help shoppers find the right store.

Not all shops plan to make money. NASA has a site from which you can down-load photographs of space. If you want to know the DNA sequence that describes all of humanity, you can find the parts scientists have already figured out through the Human Genome Project, which keeps its results on the Web.

### End of strained Cyberspace metaphor describing the Web

But you . . . you want to make money (which presumably explains why you bought the book you're currently holding) and that means you have a strong interest in how to use the Web commercially.

Before we focus on selling techniques, we have a few other practical matters to cover. Here's one: once somebody has decided to buy from you, how can you help them do so?

# Secure Transactions on the World Wide Web

A lot of research and development money has gone into helping companies provide shoppers with a secure way to order merchandise and pay for it without exposing themselves to the risk of credit card fraud.

To be absolutely blunt, most of what you read about hackers, Internet security holes, and all the rest amounts to little more than unwarranted hysteria.

Yes, really good hackers (actually *crackers*—the term *hacker* refers to extraordinarily adept programmers good enough to disassemble—hack—complex programs to figure out what's in them) can break through even sophisticated security schemes to goof around, steal information, or perform other bits of nastiness, including the creation of fraudulent credit card transactions. So what?

People provide credit card numbers to total strangers over the telephone, not worrying about how easy it is to tap a phone. They read them over cordless phones, not worrying about how extraordinarily easy it is to eavesdrop on a cordless phone. They read them over cellular phones, when prisoners attend informal workshops on how to turn a cellular phone into a cellular scanner for less than $500.

Heck, people fax order forms to catalog companies, which means their credit card information sits in plain view of large numbers of underpaid telemarketers.

So why all the hype about insecure Internet transactions? First, it makes good press. The thought of antisocial, nerdy creatures sitting at their computers at 3 A.M., eating cold pizza and cracking into corporate computers to transfer large sums of money into their personal bank accounts gets people's attention.

Second, computer programmers don't think like normal people. They don't think, "We need to make electronic commerce on the Internet as secure as the kinds of commerce people participate in now." Programmers think, "We need to make electronic commerce on the Internet perfect so nobody, under any imaginable set of circumstances, can possibly steal even a penny."

So far, absolutely perfect security has eluded the Internet because, as you'll recall, the people who built it didn't think in terms of security. They thought in terms of open and easy access. What were they thinking of?

Still, perception has more power than reality, and the average consumer reads more about nefarious hackers breaking into credit files through the Internet than about more common, prosaic forms of fraud.

The "net" result (sorry!): right now, few companies even offer to accept orders through the Internet. Instead, they provide a toll-free number so consumers can purchase through far less convenient, less secure phone lines.

But take heart: perfection, or at least a new level of secure transactions, will arrive very shortly. Secure transactions on the Net take one of two forms: encrypted transactions and digital cash.

For those readers who only speak Marketing, the word *encryption* refers to the process of translating a message from readable form, called plaintext, to a garbled, jumbled, incomprehensible form called ciphertext. *Decryption* refers to the process that translates ciphertext back to plaintext.

Encryption appeals to the Internet community because it lets anyone communicate privately (a good thing in the Internet culture) over an open, unrestricted (another good thing) communication channel, without requiring any external supervision or regulation (bad things, given the libertarian flavor of the Net).

Encrypted transactions require customers to enter a credit card number along with the rest of the ordering information. Then, using any of several commercially available encryption systems, a ciphertext version of the order wends its way through the Internet to create a transaction in the seller's order-entry system after first going through the decryption process.

Digital cash also requires encryption, but works more like a debit card than a credit card. Buyers transfer money into an on-line cash account managed by one of several service bureaus—on-line banks, really—that have entered this business. Because only those funds transferred into the buying account can be withdrawn, buyers have an automatic additional layer of protection when using digital cash.

Digital cash has another advantage, which may not be obvious.

Most of us think in terms of marketing tangible objects. When selling a tangible thing to a buyer, we all naturally gravitate to processing credit card transactions and sending back a product (for a fee to handle shipping and handling costs). The absolute best stuff to sell on the Web can exist as bits and bytes, which can transfer directly from the seller's computer to the buyer's computer . . . for a price.

## FIGURE 1-1

*Yahoo! is one of the better-known online directories. It acts as both a Table of Contents and searchable Index. Any company doing business on the World Wide Web should register its URL with every directory it can find. In this instance, asking Yahoo! to find references to "Silicon Graphics" resulted in 48 matches.*

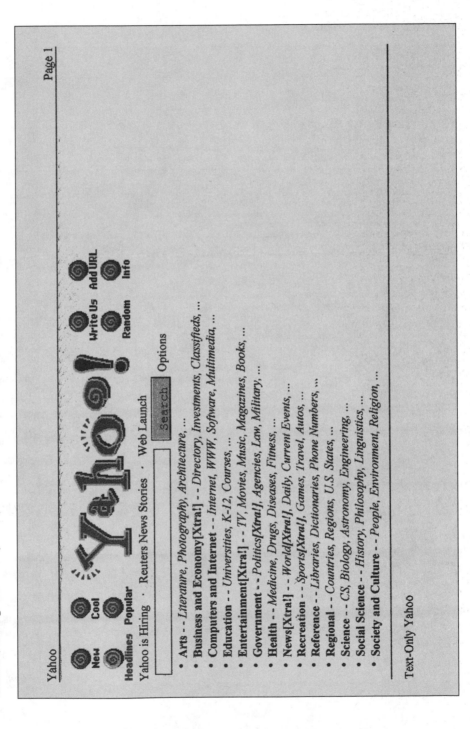

**FIGURE 1–1 (Continued)**

## Yahoo Search Results

Found 48 matches containing **silicon graphics**. Displaying matches 1-25.
Business and Economy:Companies:Computers:Systems:Workstations:**SiliconGraphics**
Business and Economy:Companies:Computers:Systems:Workstations:**SiliconGraphics:Silicon** Studio

Arts:Computer Generated:**Graphics**
- **SiliconGraphics** - The Gallery - Contains **graphics** and 3D images for your viewing pleasure! Most of these images have come from SGI customers and partners.
- **Silicon** Space - Homepage with various images, animations, cool links and **graphics** information.

Business and Economy:Companies:Computers:Multimedia
- Electromedia, Inc - We use **SiliconGraphics** Workstations, the most power ful platform used for 3D modeling, rendering and animation.

Business and Economy:Companies:Computers:Peripherals:Resellers
- Falcon Systems Inc - UNIX peripherals designed to enhance SUN, **SiliconGraphics**, Hewlett-Packard, Digital & IBM platforms.

Business and Economy:Companies:Computers:Resellers
- Stellar Technology - We design, sell, and support turnkey solutions using Hewlett Packard, IBM, Motorola, **SiliconGraphics**, Inc, and Sun hardware running Accugraph, Adobe, Alias/Wavefront and Hewlett Packard software.
- Video Images Inc. - a reseller of professional and industrial video equipment like Sony, computer equipment like **Silicon Graphics** and Optibase MPEG encoders, and other related products.

Business and Economy:Companies:Computers:Software:Consulting:Cookware
- Cookware - cookware provides **SiliconGraphics** development work and solutions for other Unix workstations and DOS based machines. Our custom software is developed to strict guidelines, and boasts of a 3:1 documentation to code ratio.

Business and Economy:Companies:Computers:Software:**Graphics**
- Easy Software Products - small software company based in Maryland that develops 2D and 3D software for **SiliconGraphics** workstations.
- National Pixel Products - National Pixel Products has been a supplier of professional-quality 2D and 3D **graphics** and animation tools for **SiliconGraphics**, Sun, and Apple Macintosh systems since 1987.
- **SiliconGraphics@**

Business and Economy:Companies:Computers:Software:Modeling, Simulation, and Visualization:Easy Software Products
- Easy Software Products - three-dimensional modeling tools for **SiliconGraphics**, Inc. workstations.

Business and Economy:Companies:Computers:Software:Multimedia
- Integrated Research - developer of media integration tools for **SiliconGraphics** workstation. Integrated Video is the comprehensive video and animation systems integration software.
- Interactive Effects Web Outpost - a developer of high end paint and **graphics** software for **SiliconGraphics** workstations.

Business and Economy:Companies:Computers:System Integrators
- Micro Madness, Ltd. - Resellers of Apple and **SiliconGraphics** workstations for Internet, publishing, multimedia/video markets. Offer cross-platform integration, turn-key Web solutions, web serving, networking, consulting and training.

Business and Economy:Companies:Computers:Systems:Supercomputers
- **SiliconGraphics@**

Business and Economy:Companies:Computers:Systems:Workstations:**SiliconGraphics**
- Center for Visual Creation at MsState.Edu - A **SiliconGraphics** National Training Center
- Nihon **SiliconGraphics**
- **SiliconGraphics**
- **SiliconGraphics** Europe
- **SiliconGraphics** FTP Server
- **SiliconGraphics** Germany
- **SiliconGraphics** Taiwan

Business and Economy:Companies:Computers:Systems:Workstations:**SiliconGraphics:Silicon** Studio
- **Silicon** Studio

Next 23 matches

# 2 Your Internet Communications Goals

Is a puzzlement.

Here we have, at last, the first truly interactive medium. In theory, the Internet should approach, in one-to-one relationships, the personal link grocers had with our grandmothers. "Mrs. Jones," they'd say, "I know you want this cut of meat. And we just got in some fresh strawberries. Mr. Jones loves those strawberries, doesn't he?"

Those may have been golden times for interactive relationships, but they were doomed because true one-to-one can't make any money.

So here is our twenty-first century replacement, and what are we doing? We're as dispassionate and removed as the faceless cashier at the supermarket checkout counter.

Don't assume for a minute we need new technology to greet surfers . . . potential customers . . . on a one-to-one level. That technology is simple. Don't assume for a minute we can't acknowledge that rarity on the Internet—an actual order!—with personalized enthusiasm. This has nothing to do with technology. It's the basic blend of courtesy and psychology absent from the psyches of cold-blooded technicians who control so much Internet communication.

And by "technician" we don't mean the visionary engineers who built the Internet without any encouragement from the hordes of marketing majors too busy to bother with computer-related media.

Not at all. We're talking about formulaic, statistics-obsessed marketers and advertisers more preoccupied with "being cool" than with clearly defining and achieving useful business goals. Technicians mistake means for ends, and so mistake technique for creativity.

And the Web should be the home of creative marketing. Let's start by looking at why companies decide—and why they *should* decide—to establish a presence on the Web.

Probably the most common (and most poorly chosen) reason is ego. Somehow, a company decides it *ought* to be on the Web, so it throws together a bunch of stuff, puts up a home page, and wonders why nobody shows up. Since form follows function, let's do better by putting some thought into why a business might want to put up a Web site.

The Coca-Cola "Sports and Entertainment" site (Fig. 2–1) typifies neutral presences. The surfer notes it, is not annoyed by it, but may see little reason to revisit.

# Web Strategies

Here are some useful business models in evidence today on the Web:

**Customer Service → Stronger Relationship →**

**Customer Retention and Upselling**

Right now, companies get more bang per buck using the Web for customer service than for any other purpose. Software companies let customers download software fixes. Airlines provide flight schedules. Manufacturers of all kinds provide product specifications. For example, see Figure 2–2, Kodak. The illustrations in this book don't carry you all the way through the site, but you can see how much information is available. Note also the special advantage of a Web presence. The individual can quickly bypass the encyclopedic amounts of information that offer no interest and click on areas of interest for as much information as he or she could possibly want.

Television networks and movie studios set up Web sites for popular programs and movies. Direct marketing agencies provide reprints of articles giving helpful advice on how to market. And every single one, or at least every business with an ounce of sense (or gram of sense, if you use the metric system) gives the customer a way to talk back.

Figure 2–3, a Microsoft page, shows yet another variation of generating interest and thus frequent revisits. Pages are customized to appeal to different viewer interests and change daily, providing a reason to come back again and again to see what's new.

When you consider that in most business-to-business environments each customer a company retains matches five new customers, you begin to understand how valuable a low-cost, high-convenience medium like the Web can be for enhancing customer service. Existing customers have already decided to buy from you. So long as you keep them, you automatically generate new sales.

### Useful Information  →  Increased Consumption  →  More Purchases

Many companies, in particular those that sell through retail channels, use Web sites to provide useful information that includes new uses for their products. The result: pre-sold customers. Among the other excellent characteristics of Ragu's Web site, its hundreds of Ragu-oriented recipes provide visitors with reasons to return and reasons to buy more Ragu. (See Fig. 2–3.)

## Convenient Buying + Discounts + Direct Sales + Reduced Overhead

The most challenging, measurable, and financially rewarding use of the Web is to directly generate sales. Whether you provide an on-screen order form or a toll-free number, making your cash register ring is the ultimate goal of all marketing. If your products lend themselves to direct sales, don't be bashful. They're visiting your home page. Persuade them to buy!

## New Entertainment/Information Dimension → Increased Product Involvement → Repeat Business or Enhanced Perceived Value

Media companies have started to use this strategy with great success. Newspaper and magazine publishers use Web sites to enhance their customers' involvement with their print products. The Web lets them serve small communities of interest and also offers opportunities for interactivity far beyond a *Letters-to-the-Editor* page. The result: increased customer loyalty.

Movie studios set up home pages for popular (or hoped-to-be popular) efforts. Since studios depend on repeat business for profitability (how many times did you see *Star Wars* or *Close Encounters*?), Web sites that offer interactivity, plot and character background, information about the actors, director and producer, and other factoids that let visitors think of themselves as part of the *cognoscenti* can't help but drive ticket sales.

Television studios pursue a similar strategy: People who watch *The X-Files* now have an *X-Files* home page to visit. The result? They're less likely to miss an episode and more likely to talk up the show to their friends. After all, they know something their friends don't, giving them bragging rights.

## Brand Enhancement → Customer Loyalty + Improved Margins

Companies that have active brand-management strategies build Web sites designed to reinforce their overall image. Levi

Strauss (Figure 2–6), Coca Cola, Nike, all use the Web for this purpose.

Opinion: of all the uses for the Web, this one has the smallest payoff. The good news: since nobody can tell if you've succeeded or failed, this strategy works well in highly political environments.

### Database Marketing

Want the names of a group of loyal, enthusiastic customers? Find a way to capture the identities, demographics, and interests of everyone who visits your Web site. The Web is an ideal medium for database development, since you can get your customers to directly update your database. Regardless of your main strategy, you can piggyback a database marketing strategy on top of it.

## WHAT WILL WORK FOR YOU?

To choose the best of these strategies, you first need to think about why potential customers might come in for a visit.

So let's take a look at *why* readers or surfers or whatever we might choose to call them are in the Internet as potential shoppers. Come to think of it, let's agree on terms that make sense within the parameters of this book: When they're casually browsing the Net, they're surfers. When you've stopped them long enough to make a sales pitch, they're *potential customers*. When they've chosen your home page because they regularly buy from you now, they're *current customers*.

# Types of Cybernaut

Whenever you're selling, you need to understand the experiential framework of the buyer. This universal truth holds just as much importance in cyberspace as it does in a shoe store. And just as in the shoe store, customers differ. By understanding those differences, you can do a far better job of tailoring your Web site to the surfers, potential customers, and/or current customers you most care to serve.

So how do we categorize those who meander around the World Wide Web?

## DIRECTED INFORMATION SEEKERS

The Internet provides access to an astonishing volume of information. Regardless of your subject, you can find both archival and up-to-the-minute information.

Need to know the DNA sequence associated with muscular dystrophy? It's almost certainly there on the Web. The reason the dinosaur we used to call *Brontosaurus* now goes by the moniker *Apatosaurus?* It's probably there too.

Need a copy of the story your local newspaper ran on your competitor last month? If your newspaper has an on-line edition, you'll probably find the article you need, ready for you to peruse at your leisure.

Directed information seekers are looking for a particular piece of information. If you have it, they want to visit your site. If you don't, they want to find out as fast as they can, so they can move on to another possible source.

Do current and potential customers regularly call you wanting more information about your products? If so, you can do your customers, and yourself, a big favor: make that information available on the Web.

## UNDIRECTED INFORMATION SEEKERS

Some people just find lots of different things interesting. Today, they want to know whether Mars hosts any life forms. Tomorrow, they're concerned about the Ebola virus. The next day they'll want to know about Intel's next chip, or maybe about how Leonardo da Vinci mixed his paint pigments.

Have something interesting to say? You'll probably grab this group's attention.

## BARGAIN HUNTERS

No, not discount shoppers. We're talking about the group that's heard about all of the fabulous free stuff you can get on the Internet. They're constantly on the lookout for free software, free photographs, free books . . . free anything.

Have something you can give away as a premium? You'll get their attention. Then you have to convert them into paying customers. That's a principal purpose of this book.

## ENTERTAINMENT SEEKERS

As a nation, we're probably more obsessed with avoiding boredom than any other on earth. Nothing to do on a Friday night? Let's take a spin on the Web!

Nobody knows how long the phenomenon will last, but for the time being the Web has become an entertainment medium. You can find interactive games and contests, "cool" corporate sites (never mind if there's any point to them!), personal Web pages, horoscopes, recipes, sex, drugs, and rock 'n' roll.

## DIRECTED BUYERS

A directed buyer wants to buy something. Now. She may have a particular item in mind—a Beer-of-the-Month Club membership, or maybe some flowers. Or, he may be behind in his holiday shopping and is looking for an idea on what to buy for his mother-in-law, who already has two of everything she's ever wanted.

Make sure you can cater to this group. Make the ordering process as easy as possible. Make sure you provide separate buyer and shipping addresses. Provide an ideas page, an interactive shopping helper, or at least a searchable product database . . . something to help a visitor find the right item in your catalog.

If you're adventurous, have a techie build software that analyzes an order and suggests a complementary item.

# Why Do People Shop in Cyberspace?

Those who have the hookup—and as of this writing, they still are a fraction of the potential universe—obviously also have the option. Just about every Internet presence also has a persona elsewhere.

Why—under what circumstances—would anyone choose the Internet for news instead of opening *the same daily newspaper* he or she seeks out on the Net? Why would anyone spend Internet time seeking out a magazine whose printed pages probably are far easier to find and read?

Why would a surfer ignore the flood of catalogs coming to his/her door and instead poke around the Net looking for bargains and surprises?

That last word is half the answer: *Surprises*. The other half is *immediacy*.

The medium's immediacy generates two more Net advantages: searchableness (the computer does the search for you), and convenience. You don't have to go searching for the catalog that came in the mail last week, the one you stuck in a pile someplace for later. The Net is there when you want it.

The Net is *right now*, far beyond any other media "now"-ness (except for an occasional "You are there" episode, such as the celebrated 1994 O. J. Simpson freeway ride). Who wouldn't want to read a weekly newsmagazine three days before it hits the stands and mailboxes? Who wouldn't want to get an advance peek into the pages of a catalog the post office will take another twelve days to deliver?

So why don't more Net advertisers exploit the now-ness? Three answers come from those who don't:

1. What we sell isn't in that category.

2. We don't want to ruin our core business by competing with ourselves.

3. Screaming isn't dignified.

These answers open up another question: Do these marketers belong on the Net at all? For that matter, do companies that timid belong in business at all? "What we sell isn't in that category" is an excuse for inaction. "We don't want to ruin our core business by competing with ourselves" is defeatist because if they don't compete, a competitor will. "Screaming isn't dignified" is a loser both ways: Either don't scream or don't worry about dignity.

Unsuccessful marketing is the least dignified result any campaign could suffer, isn't it?

- Are you building a relationship? Or are you bypassing a relationship?

- Are you saying, "Here's Something for You"? Or "Read This Because I'm Here"?

If you still wonder how so many sophisticated, big-budget advertisers are shooting blanks on the Internet, don't. These companies (and obviously the individuals who run them) are advertisers, not marketers, and they're on the Internet either because they think form equals substance, or because they're afraid not to be. The key point to make is that they don't really know why they're on the Net.

Figure 2–4 is Ragu, whose URL is *www.eat.com.* For the web surfer, Ragu's presentation is a visual (and auditory) feast.

Ragu's presence is a model of second-generation Internet

marketing—what we call "salesworthy edutainment." The home page is called Mama's Cucina. In keeping with second-generation understanding of the typical Web surfer's mindset, the home page is bright and peppy without taking much time to download.

The surfer has choices:

- Cookbook

- What's New at Mama's

- Goodies from Mama,

- "Phrases from Professor Antonio,"

- A contest (an involvement technique)

Notice the cleverness of "Phrases from Professor Antonio," Italian-language statements in both print and sound (for surfers who have multimedia computers). Some are conversation pieces, such as "How do you say 'Joe Green' in Italian?" (Giuseppe Verdi.) A number of happy quotes relate to Ragu, and changing these daily or weekly obviously is easy, overcoming a primary Internet paradox: the need for frequent updating and the labor-intensive nature of frequent updating. An example of the phrases:

**"Quella salsa pizzica come il sole siciliano"** . . .

which means, "That spicy Red Pepper Sauce is as hot as the Sicilian sun."

The contest, too, was structured to change regularly. One contest was called "Win a Family Reunion from Mama"; another was "Win a Trip to Italy."

Notice these contests are *not* contests-for-the-sake-of-contests. Ragu ties each one to its products. To enter a contest, all one does is enter his/her e-mail address and then the genuine name and address, plus some basic demographic information such as age-range.

Voila! Ragu gets an enriched database. The surfer gives Ragu implicit permission to correspond via e-mail. Another surfer option: notification when Ragu runs coupons in the paper or introduces a new product.

All of this reinforces the points made earlier about different Web strategies.

Compare Ragu with Delta Airlines, whose early presence on the Net seemed both stiff and uncomfortable. The surfer clicked into "Delta Dream Vacations" and here, as of this writing, is the exact wording the surfer encountered:

> The name Delta DREAM VACATIONS is your assurance of the highest standard in leisure travel. From check-in to check-out, your vacation experience is backed by the quality of a name you can trust. For years, Delta Air Lines has been recognized as a leader in customer satisfaction. We take our position in the travel market very seriously. That's why we are sure that Dream Vacations are developed in conjunction with the most respected names in the industry.

The message has a near-zero correlation with any of the typical surfer demographics, psychographics, or attitudes at time of surfing.

> The arrow keys move down the page to the next item:
> At Delta DREAM VACATIONS, we pay attention to detail. So you can pay attention to having fun. And simply can count on our superior service, experience and quality anywhere you travel.
> Take a look at the benefits of a Delta DREAM VACATION.

Problem: Interjecting a marching-in-place introduction damages the slight curiosity and slighter interest a surfer may have prior to hitting the site. The creative team should ask: If we were surfers instead of advertisers, would we really want to look further after exposure to cliché-driven nonspecifics?

Subsequently, Delta's "SkyLinks" site became a model of

cross-postings and cross-promotions; but Delta's "Plane Fun— London Skyscrapers" entry (Figure 6–1C) seemed to offer an unnamed prize in exchange for a considerable amount of time.

# Follow the Golden Rule of Sales Letter-Writing

One of the most valuable (in terms of response) rules any direct response letter-writer learns is:

### Fire a big gun to start the battle.

Oh, how that applies to the Net! You're at point-blank range when the surfer first lands on your site. Fire! You'll be lucky to ever have that quick closeness again, especially if you're firing blanks or trying to knock over the surfer with a sponge.

Will the need for a powerful first blast decrease as the Net matures? Probably not. It hasn't in any other medium.

The Internet isn't a magazine with a finite number of pages that a traveler picks up on an airplane. It isn't a television show which, entertaining or not, will end two minutes before the hour. It isn't a piece of direct mail, whose components the recipient can skim, scanning and/or discarding piecemeal. Here are tens of thousands of sites, and the surfer is king or queen in an endless domain. The desire to explore, to seek out a site unvisited before, is greater than the desire to retrace earlier steps *unless* something, SOMETHING at a previously-visited site calls the surfer back with the power of a siren song.

That's the challenge. And that's why *marketers* have a definite edge over *advertisers* and a major edge over the term-throwers and the technicians and the intruders from the world of "conventional" advertising whose goals don't parallel those of marketers because they aren't able to think of themselves as one-to-one salespeople.

Entertainment can bring people back to you. But does it bring them back as buyers? Absolutely, so long as you're selling entertainment in the first place. Otherwise *edutainment*, a *marketing* invention for the Net, can be a happy compromise bridging both philosophical worlds. Figure 2–7, The Dilbert Store, exemplifies this unique Net capability.

Before you leave this chapter, take some time to look over Figure 2–4, Ragu, an inspired use of the Web for *edutainment*. Aside from its brightness and its remarkable combination of entertainment and product relevance, this site gives the visitor an opportunity to *interact*.

That wonderful term *Lifetime Value* is never so wonderful as when it applies to somebody who has responded to *your* message. What might be the lifetime value of a Ragu visitor who, knowing (for example) the written/spoken Italian phrases change frequently, becomes a Ragu enthusiast?

# Building a Relationship on the Net

If you're a pussyfooter, afraid of your promotional shadow, response to your Internet message will disappoint you, just as the weakness of impact will disappoint those who see it and wander off elsewhere in search of greater titillation.

In business as in personal lives, the foundation of a dynamic relationship is a dynamic presence. You want a surfer to say to friends, "Hey, have you seen that site?" Being the discoverer of an exciting, truly interactive site brings with it the loyalties and fealty marketers dream of.

But careful, please:

We can see the wrong conclusion forming; *Let's startle . . . let's shock. Let's astonish. That'll grab 'em.*

Yes, it will. But it won't build the kind of relationship a *marketer* wants to build, because the surfer then views you as either a show-off or as comic relief, not as a logical supplier.

So the governor on the throttle has to be a solid recognition of why you're on the Net, what your customers—those surfers who have an interest in your product or service—will respond favorably to, and what you're trying to get them to do.

## THE PERFECT MEDIUM FOR QUESTIONS

A huge advantage the Net has over traditional media is its potential for exploiting its semi-synonym: *Interactive*.

Surfers don't get annoyed when a marketer asks a question. They get annoyed when marketers DON'T ask a question.

But know these two qualifiers:

- First, the question has to suggest information or benefit for the surfer, not for the marketer. Ignoring this logic is one of the principal mistakes technicians make when they usurp Internet marketing functions.

At first glance, the Money Card Collector site (Figure 2–9A) seems to violate this principle. It appears to be mere listing of issues and dealers who advertise on the site. But, actually, it meets the needs of a particular kind of surfer, who is looking for this particular kind of information. The inclusion of international dealers is a particular marketing advantage offered by the Web.

- Second, the question has to be consistent with ethical principles of marketing—preferably *direct* marketing—or you'll be one of those who adds a little more tarnish to this newest member of the communications family.

And how, you ask, can a *question* run afoul of ethical principles? By loading itself with an implied promise designed to mislead. An example is this one, singled out for attack by regulators (who will jump into Internet waters like piranhas when—no, *as*—abuses continue):

**"If you could make $10,000 in the next 30 days,
would you take 20 minutes to learn how it is done?"**

True or untrue—and obviously the regulators jumped on it because they concluded it was untrue—this one couldn't have been structured by a knowledgeable *direct* marketer, because direct marketing professionals know what a turnoff the word *learn* is.

## TECHNIQUE IS LESS SIGNIFICANT THAN POTENTIAL

Whether statement or question, promise or threat, the First Rule of Internet Advertising is a can't-miss yardstick:"

**Stop the surfer in his/her tracks.**

If you've written envelope copy for a piece of direct mail, or if you've tossed an envelope into the wastebasket because the envelope didn't "grab" you, you can see the parallel. Envelope copy is traditional media's first cousin to the First Rule of Internet Advertising.

As sites proliferate by the tens of thousands, the Rule becomes ever more profound.

**FIGURE 2–1**

*"Cool" talk is non-threatening to those who visit the Coca-Cola site. Will it help Coca-Cola's market position? The company may argue that this isn't the purpose of the site. What is?*

Hit the box office window or stadium seats and we'll kick you off into some hot sports and entertainment addresses. Or, if that doesn't melt your ice cubes, choose your own direction. And come back often - there's more cool stuff on deck, waiting to come online in the not-so-distant future.

**About The Coca-Cola Company.** Stock updates. Our mission. Even a chance to pick the brains of the way high ups.    

**Speak Your Mind.** Pontificate and ponder. Grab a gif. Forward some fun to a friend.    

**Trading Post.** The place to be for collectors, pinheads, traders and shoppers.    

**Refreshment.** As more of The Coca-Cola Company brands from countries all over the globe become Web-wise, this spot will really heat up. In the meantime, quaff some mental refreshment.    

**The World of Coca-Cola Pavilion.** Visit our exhibit du jour. Pick up some dinner-party trivia. Stop by the gift shop on the way out. And come back soon for something new.    

**It's a Mystery.** People cruise the Web because they're looking for someplace to go. Someplace Cool. Someplace Refreshing. Someplace Fun. Someplace...Else. Here are a few of our pixels.    

**The Centennial Olympic Games in Atlanta.** Since 1928, Coca-Cola and the Games have gone together. Now we want you in on all the fun.

**FIGURE 2–2A**
*Kodak doesn't waste its Web site on trivia. Clicking the computer mouse on any of the described subjects brings a torrent of information specific to that subject. Therein lies an advantage of a Web presence: Despite an impossibly huge encyclopedia of information, the individual quickly bypasses those areas of no interest and centers on areas of interest.*

Welcome to the Eastman Kodak Company

| What's New | About Kodak | Photography | Search | What's Hot |
| Product Information | Digital Imaging | Customer Solutions |

Last Update: Monday July 8, 1996 at 16:32:10 | Search | Guest Book | Site Survey |
Contact *webmaster@kodak.com* if this server presents any problems.

Earth in background image: photo credit - NASA

Copyright, Eastman Kodak Company, 1994

**FIGURE 2–2B**

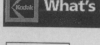 **What's New**                                              Search

*The picture is changing . . .*

Yes, the picture at Kodak is changing! We hope that you like everything here at the Kodak Web Site and
find it useful to help you make decisions about KODAK products or take <u>Great Pictures</u>! If this web site
doesn't make your life better in some way, please leave a comment in our <u>Guest Book</u>. We are seeking
talented professionals. We invite you to review our <u>Employment Opportunities</u>!

- **<u>Press Releases</u>**

- **<u>KODAK Picture Disk Software</u>** (7/3/96)
- **<u>Kodak Adds International Content</u>** (7/3/96)
- **<u>International Science and Engineering Fair</u>** (7/2/96)
- **<u>Education Technology Grant Application</u>** (7/1/96)
- **<u>Eastman Kodak Company Health, Safety and Environment 1995 Report</u>** (6/21/96)
- **<u>Eastman Kodak Company Sponsors the Rochester International Golf
  Tournament</u>** (6/19/96)
- **<u>Eastman Kodak Company Sponsors the 1996 Summer Olympics</u>** (6/19/96)
- **<u>1996 National Parks Program Schedule</u>** (6/11/96)
- **<u>Kodak Site Survey</u>** (6/10/96)
- **<u>Developers Relations Group</u>** (6/4/96)
- **<u>Scotti's World - DC20 Camera introduction</u>** (6/3/96)
- **<u>Take a survey, get a chance to win a DC20 Camera</u>** (6/3/96)
- **<u>Free - Download Picture Postcard Software</u>** (6/3/96)
- **<u>Kodak's Commitment to the DICOM Standard</u>** (5/28/96)
- **<u>Kodak Sponsors Canadian National Magazine Awards</u>** (5/3/96)
- **<u>Eastman Kodak Company 1995 Annual Report</u>** (4/30/96)
- **<u>George Fisher at the American Association of Advertising Agencies' Annual
  Meeting</u>** (4/25/96)
- **<u>Special Feature: 8650 Color Thermal Printers</u>** (4/24/96)
- Kodak, a proud sponsor of the 1996 Summer Olympics, presents:
  **<u>Serious Fun with KODAK FUN SAVER Cameras</u>**(4/12/96)

**Kodak Home Page Menu**

| <u>What's New</u> | <u>About Kodak</u> | <u>Photography</u> | <u>Search</u> | <u>What's Hot</u> |
| <u>Product Information</u> | <u>Digital Imaging</u> | <u>Customer Solutions</u> |

<u>Kodak Home Page</u> | <u>Search</u> | <u>Guest Book</u> | <u>Site Survey</u> |

**Last Update: Wednesday, 03-Jul-96 17:47:01 EDT**

**FIGURE 2–2C**

KODAK: About Kodak

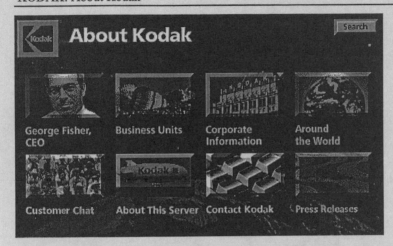

**About Kodak Menu**

- **George Fisher, CEO**
- **Business Units**
- **Corporate Information**
- **Around the World**
- **Customer Chat**
- **About This Server**
- **Contact Kodak**
- **Press Releases**

**Kodak Home Page Menu**

| What's New | About Kodak | Photography | Search | What's Hot |
| Product Information | Digital Imaging | Customer Solutions |

 Kodak Home Page | Search | Guest Book | Site Survey |

Last Update: Monday July 8, 1996 at 16:35:16
Contact _webmaster@kodak.com_ if this server presents any problems.

Copyright, Eastman Kodak Company, 1994

**FIGURE 2–3A**
*This page, by Microsoft, demonstrates how to generate frequent repeat visits by providing rapidly changing information. In this case, each visitor can customize the page to mirror particular interests, and the site automatically updates the information (stock quotes, local weather, news headlines) without any human intervention.*

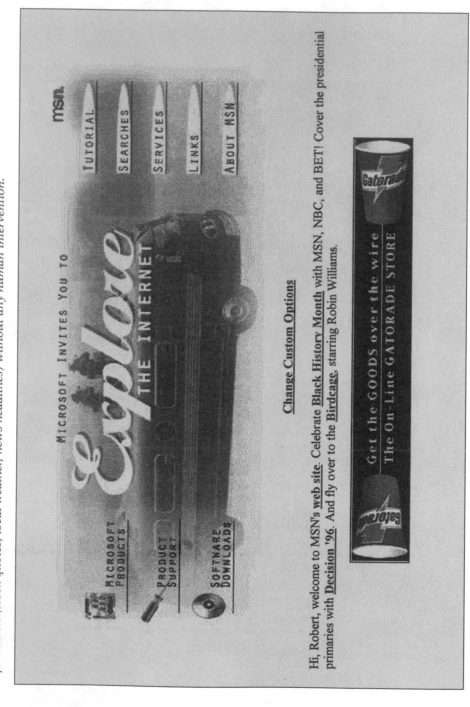

**FIGURE 2–3B**

| Stock Quotes<br>for the following:<br><br>BIOI DH CMNT | TV1<br>Free customizable TV listings |
|---|---|
| **United Media Comic Strips**<br><u>Dilbert</u> | Need more on your MSN start page? <u>Send</u> us your<br>ideas. |

**Reuters/Excite Headlines Bulletin**                    © 1996 Reuters Limited

- ☐ **Republican Candidates Press On** - The Republican presidential candidates are taking the campaign to the South and West today ahead of the next contests on the road to their party's nomination.
- ☐ **World Media Savage Buchanan** - Republican presidential candidate Pat Buchanan is being savaged by the world's media, who are dismissing his chances of winning his party's nomination.
- ☐ **Turmoil in Republican Party** - With the race for the Republican presidential nomination in turmoil, some Republican strategists and political analysts are wondering whether the party is risking lasting damage.

**Reuters/Excite Business Bulletin**                    © 1996 Reuters Limited

- ☐ **Traders Await Settled Market** - Wall Street traders are wondering if high-technology stocks will continue to dominate the market today.
- ☐ **Sears to Shed Prodigy** - Sears, Roebuck plans to unload its 50 percent stake in the Prodigy online service to focus on retailing and expansion.
- ☐ **Ameritech Seeks Expansion** - Ameritech is seeking to expand its communications services and customer base.

**Reuters/Excite International Bulletin**                    © 1996 Reuters Limited

- ☐ **Serbs Flee Sarajevo Suburbs** - Bosnian Serbs living around Sarajevo are pressing ahead today with plans to flee suburbs that are scheduled to revert to Muslim-Croat police control tomorrow.
- ☐ **Bosnia Sanctions Move Debated** - The commander of the NATO-led peacekeeping force in Bosnia has asked the United Nations to postpone a decision on lifting sanctions on Bosnian Serbs.
- ☐ **World Media Savage Buchanan** - Republican presidential candidate Pat Buchanan is being savaged by the world's media, who are dismissing his chances of winning his party's nomination.

**Weather Information**

Local Weather:

| <u>Change Custom Options</u> | <u>Send us feedback</u> |
|---|---|

<u>Text only page</u>

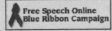

<u>Copyright</u>
© 1996 Microsoft Corporation
Image © FPG International

**FIGURE 2–4A**

*In a milieu of marketers who seem to regard the Internet as a parallel to advertising in the daily newspaper, Ragu stands out as a champion. Here is a thoughtful, salesworthy, and thoroughly appealing interactive site. Obviously, reprinting the entire site would require more space than this book allows. But you can get (and the word is apt in this usage) the flavor.*

**FIGURE 2–4B**

Button Bar

## "Mangia bene, eh!"

"I got a million delicious recipes for you. Scroll down -- you'll find something you're crazy for. Some have nice pictures. Plus, just in case you need a little extra help, I've given you a cooking glossary and a pasta glossary. Go, explore! Be the Marco Polo of the kitchen!"

"Trying to find something special but not sure where to look? Don't worry, Mama will help you search for whatever you want."

- Primi Piatti (Appetizers)
- Secondi Piatti (Main Dishes)
    - Mama's New Sauce Recipes NEW! |
    - Pastas
    - Chicken Dishes
    - Pizzas
    - Mini-Pizzas
    - Seafood
    - Beef, Pork, & Veal Dishes
    - Other Dishes
    - Light & Healthy
- Dolce (Desserts)

## I'm not sure -- Mama, you decide.

"Can't decide what to make? Come back every week and Mama will give you one of her favorites."

## Recipes
## Primi Piatti (Appetizers)
- Aioli With Fresh Vegetables
- Minestrone Soup
- Chicken-Rice Soup
- Italian Marinated Bean Salad
- Bow Tie Pasta Toss Salad NEW! |
- Spicy Eggplant Parmesan NEW! |
- Tortellini Toss NEW! |
- Chicken Dijon Potato Salad
- Chicken Tortellini Salad
- Antipasto Pasta Salad
- Broccoli Tortellini Salad

## Secondi Piatti (Main Dishes)
## Mama's New Sauce Recipes
### Pasta Toss
- Bow Tie Pasta Toss Salad

**FIGURE 2–4C**

- Tortellini Toss
- Pasta Toss Primavera
- Sausage and Broccoli Rabe Pasta Toss

### Ragú Alfredo

- Chicken With Pesto Alfredo
- Fettuccine With Broccoli Carbonara
- Tomato Alfredo Pasta
- Shrimp Alfredo

### Spicy Red Pepper

- Spicy Eggplant Parmesan
- Layered Rotini Lasagna
- Spicy Red Pepper Clam Sauce

## Pastas

- Fettuccine Primavera
- Hearty Lasagna Rolls
- Pepperoni Pasta Ruffles
- Linguini With Zucchini & Cheese
- Stuffed Shells Primavera
- Quick 'N Easy Pasta Bolognese
- Twirls Romanesque
- Garden Harvest Lasagna
- Tuscan Style Pasta
- Linguini With Pepperoni & Mushrooms
- Simply Tortellini
- Fettuccine With Broccoli Carbonara NEW!
- Layered Rotini Lasagna NEW!
- Pasta Toss Primavera NEW!
- Tomato Alfredo Pasta NEW!
- Baked Ziti With Ricotta Cheese
- Easy Vegetable Pasta
- Pasta With Beans Italiano
- Feta Fettuccine
- Spicy Shells With Vegetables
- Spaghetti With Lean Meatballs
- Seafood Pasta
- Vegetable Bow Tie Pasta
- Classic Stuffed Shells
- Linguini With Red Clam Sauce
- Pasta With Roasted Peppers
- Olive Lovers' Pasta
- Four Cheese Pasta
- Lasagna With A Twist
- Vegetable Primavera Lasagna

## Chicken Dishes

- Easy Bake Chicken Casserole
- Classic Chicken Parmesan
- Chicken With Pesto Alfredo NEW!
- Chicken With Chive Dumplings
- Mashed Potato Chicken Casserole
- Chicken Vegetable Newburg
- Chicken Vegetable Stir-Fry
- Honey Mustard Chicken Casserole
- Spicy Apricot Chicken
- Grilled Chicken Kebabs

**FIGURE 2–4D**

## Spaghetti With Lean Meatballs

- 1 pound ground turkey
- 1 egg, beaten
- 1/2 cup Italian seasoned bread crumbs
- 2 tablespoons minced fresh parsley
- 1/8 teaspoon black pepper
- 1 tablespoon olive oil
- 1 jar (27 1/2 oz.) Ragú Light Pasta Sauce
- 12 ounces spaghetti, cooked and drained
- Grated Parmesan cheese

In a large bowl, thoroughly combine ground turkey, egg, bread crumbs, parsley and pepper. Shape into 1 1/2-inch meatballs. In a large skillet, thoroughly brown meatballs on all sides in olive oil; drain fat. Add sauce; cover and simmer 30 minutes. Serve sauce and meatballs over hot spaghetti. Sprinkle with cheese.

Serves 6.

- Next Recipe
- Search Mama's Cookbook
- Mama's Cookbook
- Mama's Cucina Home Page

Mama's niece Ana, the lawyer, wrote this next part: Copyright 1995 Van den Bergh Foods, Inc. All rights reserved. Ragú, Chicken Tonight, and Pizza Quick are registered trademarks of Van den Bergh Foods, Inc.

*webmaster@eat.com*

**FIGURE 2–5A**

*As you look through a typical Ticketmaster Internet presence, you can see the obvious difference between offers loaded with specifics (including price, whose importance on the Web is tied to the reason someone visits this site) and those which seem to be generalized puffery. Which will get the phone to ring more often? This marketer's pages emphasize timeliness and excitement. Immediacy plus frequent changes bring surfers back to a previously visited site. Convivial phraseology adds reader comfort.*

**FIGURE 2–5B**

SPOTLIGHT SPECIALS

**Your TM guide to
discounts, deals,
promotions, and all
around good causes!**

## NATIONAL

**Check out <u>Mercury
Tracer's Great Ticket
Weekend Giveaway</u> and**
you could make it to first
base!

**<u>Just Kick It!</u>**

You'll be in good company
in South Florida this
summer, what with 200,000
other soccer fans gathering
to see Olympic Soccer in
Miami.
**<u>Wanna go?</u>**

**Atlanta
Welcoming the World**

If you're not in Atlanta this summer, you're doing something wrong.
<u>Let us show you around.</u>

**<u>Motorola SportsTrax
Baseball Scoreboard....</u>**

can help you win tickets to
the World Series this year.
**<u>Check out our great offer!</u>**

SPORTS TRAX
*Baseball Action Wherever You Go.*

**FIGURE 2–5C**

**4th Annual Ticketmaster Music Showcase Tour**
Unclear about your band's future? Here's your chance to be seen and heard by the music industry!
Be part of Ticketmaster's Music Showcase Tour, coming to a city near you this fall.

**Feel 20 years younger...instantly!**

<u>Return to the days of yesteryear</u> when you'd escape from reality and spend a long summer day at the fair. Where else can you eat a corndog, spit off a farris wheel and win a goldfish by throwing a dime at it? Only at the fair. And all summer long, we're going to be sending some lucky winners to state fairs around the country do all that and more!

Our Man <u>Joe Fan</u> has some pretty cool links for you- check out **Joe Fan's Cool Connections**. Visit early and often.

**"The Heart Both Breaks And Soars...." - The New York Times**

" <u>Rent</u>," the exhilarating rock opera which seemingly appeared from nowhere and received rapturous reviews is now on Broadway at the <u>Nederlander Theatre</u>.

REGIONAL

## FIGURE 2–6

*This slow-to-download page by Levi Strauss may generate a "so what?" attitude, where a quick-to-download page . . . even one lacking specific reasons for the site's existence . . . might transform a casual surfer into a short-time visitor.*

Levi Strauss & Co. - Welcome!

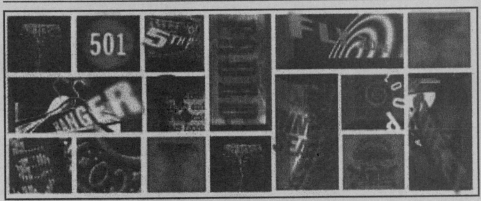

**Fly Zone**
    It's the next best thing to being there. Zone in on what's hot around the world.
**Inner Seam**
    Take a look from the inside at how we do what we do.
**Fifth Pocket**
    What's inside is always a mystery.
**Loop**
    Swing by and check out hot links to other worthy sites.
**Faded**
    Join Levi Strauss & Co. and see just how long and strange the trip has been.
**Street**
    If it's happening in the world of fashion, it happens on the Street first.
**Hanger**
    Get tangled up in blue inside the biggest walk-in closet on the Net.
**Help**
    If you need some, here's where you get it.

 Questions? Comments? Tell us what you think!

### FIGURE 2–7A

*An entertainment and marketing phenomenon, Scott Adams' Dilbert is a perfect match with dedicated surfers. This site, The Dilbert Store, is basically commercial, but to dedicated Dilbert aficionados doesn't appear to be commercial.*

Don't get lost in the teeming hordes of In-duh-viduals...

New from the House of Dogbert, The Dilbert Store is proud to present the DILBERT SOFTWEAR Fall Collection.

- ☐ **BEWARE!** Read our <u>Terms and Conditions</u> before ordering.
- ☐ <u>Shipping and Handling</u> information for domestic and international orders
- ☐ <u>Mail/Fax</u> orders are also accepted.

We are using the most recent security release for our server. For the best possible security we recommend that Netscape users upgrade to at least version 1.12 (1.22 for Windows) of the Netscape browser. If you have a previous version, you can <u>obtain the latest release from Netscape.</u>

If you experience any problems ordering through the Dilbert Store, please let us know. You can contact us directly through email at <u>dilbert-store@unitedmedia.com</u> with your questions.

If you are unable to order electronically, feel free to order using our toll-free number: **1-800-882-6450**
(International callers dial: **612-948-5434**)

### DILBERT and DOGBERT Dolls

By popular demand! Cuddly Dogbert and Dilbert dolls for your office, den, boat, or RV. Guaranteed to ward off pesky in-duh-viduals.

| TYPE | PRICE | QUANTITY |
|---|---|---|
| DILBERT | $22.00 | |
| DOGBERT | $22.00 | |

**FIGURE 2–7B**

### DNRC T-Shirt

Proudly proclaim your membership in Dogbert's New Ruling Class with an official DNRC cotton t-shirt.

| SIZE | PRICE | QUANTITY |
|------|-------|----------|
| L | $20.00 | |
| XL | $20.00 | |
| XXL | $21.50 | SOLD OUT |

### DNRC Cap

A perfect complement to the entire DILBERT SOFTWEAR collection, the one size fits all baseball hat features an embroidered DNRC logo on the front and a bold red and white Dilbert logo on the back.

| SIZE | PRICE | QUANTITY |
|------|-------|----------|
| One Size | $18.00 | |

### Dilbert Desk Art

Limited edition reprints of four classic Dilbert strips: King of the Cubicle, Unix, Time Line and That Computer. Numbered, framed and in a special gift box for that special someone.

| STRIP | PRICE | QUANTITY |
|-------|-------|----------|
| King of the Cubicle | $32.00 | |
| Unix | $32.00 | |
| Time Line | $32.00 | |
| That Computer | $32.00 | |

**FIGURE 2–7C**

### The New Dilbert Book

An overwhelming bestseller, the latest DILBERT collection features classic strips from 1991 and 1992. Softcover 8 1/2" x 10 7/8" format.

| BOOK | PRICE | QUANTITY |
|------|-------|----------|
| It's Obvious You Won't Survive by Your Wits Alone | $12.95 | |

### Reprint Collector's Pack

A specially priced set of the most popular DILBERT strip collections: *Bring Me the Head of Willy the Mailboy* (1995), *Shave the Whales* (1994) and *Always Postpone Meetings With Time-Wasting Morons* (1992). Softcover 8" x 8" format. Titles sold as a bundle only. (This bundle is shipped and billed as one item.)

| BUNDLE | PRICE | QUANTITY |
|--------|-------|----------|
| Reprint Collector's Pack | $24.95 | |

**FIGURE 2–7D**

### Original Works Collector's Pack

Two of the most popular original (i.e. not published in newspapers) DILBERT books in a specially priced set: Dogbert's Big Book of Business, *Build a Better Life by Stealing Office Supplies* (1991), and his official guide to ettiquette in the 90's, *Dogbert's Clues for the Clueless* (1993). Softcover 8" x 8" format. Titles sold as a pair only. (This bundle is shipped and billed as one item.)

| BUNDLE | PRICE | QUANTITY |
|---|---|---|
| Original Works Collector's Pack | $14.95 | |

### DILBERT Day-to-Day calendar

Now back in stock! The Dilbert daily desk calendar features 366 tear-off pages, each featuring a great Dilbert strip.

| CALENDAR | PRICE | QUANTITY |
|---|---|---|
| Day to Day calendar | $9.95 | |

# FIGURE 2–8

*Here is the site for a not-for-profit organization. Unless the visitor already is interested in the Fund's goals—which are presented in generalized terms—impact is minimal.*

GLOBAL TEAM     YOUR HELP     PROGRAMS

*We are committed to giving flexible, timely support to women's groups working on emerging, controversial or difficult issues.*

LINKS     GLOBAL FUND FOR WOMEN     NETWORK NEWS     F.A.Q.     OUR NEW VIDEO

Global Team | Your Help | Programs | Links | Network News | F.A.Q. | Our New Video

The GLOBAL FUND FOR WOMEN is an international organization which focuses on female human rights. It supports issues as diverse as literacy, domestic violence, economic autonomy, and the international trafficking of women, among others. It supports women's groups based outside of the U.S.

The GLOBAL FUND FOR WOMEN'S mission is to:

Listen to the concerns of women's groups globally;
Provide women's groups with financial and other resources;
Increase support for women's efforts globally;
Develop and strengthen links among women's groups worldwide;
Heighten awareness of the needs and strengths of women.

The Global Fund for Women was established in 1987 as a non-profit corporation engaged in philanthropic work; it has public charity, non-taxable, 501(c)(3) status in the United States.

*GFW*

*The Global Fund for Women*
*2480 Sand Hill Road, Suite 100*
*Menlo Park, California 94025-6941 USA*

*Telephone: (415) 854-0420*
*Fax: (415) 854-8050*
*Email: gfw@igc.apc.org*

**FIGURE 2–9A**

*The Money Card Collector site might seem, at first glance, to be nothing more than a listing of issues and dealers who advertise in both the publication and its Web site. But that, after all, is the rationale behind this site's existence. Many visitors arrive as the result of having entered a key phrase such as "Money Card" on a search engine. Listings such as these are exactly what they want. (Notice the inclusion of international dealers, a marketing advantage peculiar to the Web.)*

**Welcome to MONEYCARD Collector Magazine**

America's First Debit & Phonecard Hobby Publication On the Web

- **Current Issue Highlights**

- **Sales Manager Position Available**

- **Recent Dealer Listings**

- **"Using Modems with Phonecards"**

- **Back Issues:**

  - ☐ Volume 2, Number 9: October 1995
  - ☐ Volume 2, Number 9: September 1995
  - ☐ Volume 2, Number 8: August 1995
  - ☐ Volume 2, Number 7: July 1995
  - ☐ Volume 2, Number 6: June 1995
  - ☐ Volume 2, Number 5: May 1995
  - ☐ Volume 2, Number 4: April 1995
  - ☐ Volume 2, Number 3: March 1995
  - ☐ Volume 2, Number 2: February 1995
  - ☐ Volume 2, Number 1: January 1995
  - ☐ Volume 1, Number 4: December 1994
  - ☐ Volume 1, Number 3: November 1994
  - ☐ Volume 1, Number 2: October 1994
  - ☐ Volume 1, Number 1: September 1994

**FIGURE 2–9B**

● **Moneycard Prepaid Phonecard Faqs**

  ☐ Faq One
  ☐ Faq Two

● **Moneycard Hot Links**

  ☐ HT Technologies

**INTERNET SUBSCRIBERS ONLY:** If you subscribe to MONEYCARD Collector and mention that you read about us on the Internet, you will receive a **free copy of our first issue, Volume 1 Number 1.** This offer applies only to new subscriptions. Receive 12 issues, plus your Internet bonus, Volume 1, Number 1, for $19.95 (Non-USA subscribers add $18.00).

To subscribe, call (800) 645-7456 or
send email to: *mchurch@erinet.com*

Copyright © 1994 - 1995 Amos Press, Inc. All Rights Reserved

Back to the Phonecard Index
Back to the HyperMedia Main Topic Index
Updated: October 3, 1995

**FIGURE 2–9C**

## MONEYCARD Collector Magazine

### OCTOBER ISSUE DEALER LISTING

Moneycard Collector is designed to meet the emerging needs of phone card collectors and users. Listed below are dealer names, addresses, phone/fax numbers and specialties. If you are interested in knowing more about prepaid phone and debit cards, or are interested in buying or selling cards, please contact one of the dealers below.

## ARIZONA

| | |
|---|---|
| **PATCO**<br>P O Box 7702<br>Phoenix AZ 85011<br>Phone: (800) 408-3445<br>Fax: (602) 946-3267 | Offering a large selection of Sci-Fi, Fantasy, & Comic Phone cards. See our ad on page 49. |
| **Promotional Phone Cards**<br>1923 Cottonwood Circle<br>Mesa, AZ 85202<br>Phone: (602) 820-3102 | We carry Sport phone cards, Sprint, Assets, Disney, Coke, Pac Bell, Hawaii, GTE, AmeriVox. See our ad on page 25. |

## CALIFORNIA

| | |
|---|---|
| **A&K Telecards**<br>397 Jeannie Way<br>Livermore, CA 94550<br>Phone: (510) 447-8236<br>Fax: (510) 443-7647 | Specializing in McDonalds, Coca Cola trading Cards & inserts. |
| **American National Phone Card**<br>5959 Tampa Avenue | Specializing in Unique, Innovative & Low Mintage |

# 3 How the Internet Differs from Other Direct Marketing Media

Of all the mass communications media ever to appear, the Internet is the one most likely to change.

Its immediate predecessor, television, claimed a universality of appeal from its first days. TV had (and has) something for everyone. No member of the family is excluded. No individual says, "There's no point in my watching this medium," because of a specialized business activity.

Oh, yes, specialized business activities eliminate television as a media buy for specialized business-to-business advertisers. But even that exclusion is thinning as cable and specialty programming open "vertical" avenues of communication.

## Communicate with Whom?

The Internet was and is the most complex medium of communication ever devised. Terminology is formidable—a natural consequence of a rapidly evolving technology. In fact, marketing is a late addition to Internet action. And the medium is evolving so fast any rules can be obsolete before you even have a chance to study them.

That's because the Internet hasn't yet made up its mind what it wants to be.

How can it, when between eighty and ninety percent of our usual marketing targets haven't ever set an electronic foot on the Internet turf? Here we have an amalgam of Yellow Pages, classified advertising, "vertical" display advertising and outdoor advertising. No medium can be all things to all people. Or can it?

Look at Ore-Ida's home page (Figure 3–1A). It includes products, information about the company, and recruitment advertising in one place. While not a particularly exciting site, it illustrates the Web's ability to serve multiple nonconflicting markets in a single site. Better, cross-promotions in other media can lead visitors directly to pages inside the site. For example, a magazine advertisement for Ore-Ida's food products could refer to *http://www.orei-da.com/tatertots/* (in the upper right-hand corner of Figure 3–1B), making that the home page so far as readers of that magazine ad were concerned.

# The Odd Coupling

While, in one sense, the Net is unlike any previous communications medium, in other ways it parallels other traditional selling media.

## YELLOW PAGES

The Internet resembles Yellow Pages advertising in that the potential customer has to come looking for the advertiser. Dominance becomes impossible unless that advertiser uses other media to announce an Internet presence. Is heavy use of ancillary media to promote the primary medium a logical expenditure of advertising dollars? Traditionalists say no, although the technique of cross-promotion has been well-established. For example, *The Reader's Digest* and Publishers Clearing House use television to draw attention to their direct mail campaigns.

But what a difference! Advertising for *The Reader's Digest* in direct mail or on television isn't face-to-face with competing magazines. Compare that with the potential buyer who takes a Yellow Pages directory in hand and who may phone "AAA-Aron" because that's the first listing in the category. One result for sure: Your Yellow Pages advertising exists in the most competitive ambience in the entire world of advertising. You're surrounded by competitors pitching the same product or service you're pitching.

## CLASSIFIED ADVERTISING

How about classified? Same problem.

Well, not entirely. Along with the problem is an advantage: You *know* the person seeing your classified ad has come looking for just such an ad. Courtship is unnecessary: Your classified ad can and should launch into an immediate hard, logical sell.

More than that: It has to grab and shake the reader fast, or on goes the eye to the next ad.

So having a home page on the Internet is no assurance of visitors approaching you, even to take a peek. The parallel with Yellow Pages and classified advertising *demands* a type of creative treatment we'll explore in Chapter Five.

## DISPLAY ADVERTISING

"Vertical" display advertising is advertising aimed at one specific demographic, psychographic, or professional segment. Obviously, a trade magazine's advertisers are vertical, aiming their message at the specialized interest of the reader. The nature of Internet advertising is almost identical, because the deadly time-factor can kill off a surfer who senses the message isn't aimed directly at him/her.

The American Sales Industries' Home Page (Figure 3–2) demonstrates the parallel. "PREMIUMS AND INCENTIVES WITH PROVEN SUCCESS" will have no impact on the casual surfer. A sales manager looking for sales incentives, on the other hand, will immediately latch onto this description and explore further.

## OUTDOOR ADVERTISING

So how does outdoor advertising blend into this strange stew? The answer is obvious if you've ever landed on a home page and perceived immediate boredom. Outdoor grabs you in a fast glance or is gone forever. So does the Internet.

The owners of the Beverly Hills Camera Shop understand the parallel with Outdoor advertising. Their home page (Figure 3–3) has a definite billboard feel to it, and must grab the attention of Leica enthusiasts (that is, everyone who understands quality cameras) . . . assuming the page loads fast enough.

# Other Instant Problems

Addresses aren't easy, and if a "surfer" doesn't enter a marketer's URL (see glossary of terms) in his/her computer's "Favorite Places" listing, the possibility of doing business can vanish into the huge maw of lost addresses.

No problem—for the dedicated surfer. But who is that surfer?

We use the term his/her to save space; but how many her-surfers exist?

Unfair question. Why? Because we'd have to tie the answer to now. And—as has been the history of most computer-related developments—the first generation of Internet surfers is over-whelmingly male.

Georgia Tech's GVU Center (reachable on the Net at http://www.cc.gatech.edu/user—surveys, a mouthful even for the Internet) reported in mid-1995—admittedly the first year in which the Internet could be considered a viable advertising medium—that 80 percent of Internet users were male.

That was 1995. In that same year, penetration of computers within United States households was 35 percent, which meant that two-thirds of the consumer population couldn't surf the Net no matter how badly they wanted to. The business population is even more difficult to analyze.

# Statistics Can't Lie, But They Can Be Mistaken

Let's suppose you interpret the previous paragraph this way: An advertiser on the Internet can't contact two-thirds of buying prospects.

Wrong.

You're back in the 1950s, with Madison Avenue's concept of cost-per-thousand—mass instead of class—bulk instead of quality.

Better: Ask yourself who doesn't have a computer in the house-hold. The demographic sinks. Buying power? Down. Sophistica-tion? Down. Education? Down.

Not that we have pure cream here in Internet-land. Many, many surfers have just enough disposable income to cover their online time.

That's one reason statistics need distilling.

Another is a survey by iVALS (Internet address: http://future.sri.com), coincidental with the GVU Center. This one said 64 percent of Internet users are male. That gives a boost to females from 20 percent to 36 percent, an 80 percent increase.

A third coincidental survey, by O'Reilly and Associates, attrib-uted a wide spread—17 percent to 34 percent—of Internet usage by women.

So statistics aren't particularly valuable, except as a general indicator. The general indication was and is that males outnumber females for Net-surfing. Another indication is that a surprising percentage of "males" aren't yet pubertized males, which casts a pall on their buying power.

In Chapter 11 we'll take a look at what we can expect in the year 2001 and beyond. For now, even in its just-out-of-embryo stage, the Internet is a gigantic marketplace posing a gigantic challenge. The biggest challenge is one this book will tackle:

# Converting Internet Advertisers to Internet Marketers

They aren't the same.

The difference between an advertiser and a marketer is the difference between a smooth announcer and a dedicated, successful salesperson. Which would you rather have working for you?

Many, many Web sites were and are designed by designers and technicians. Copy? What's that? The medium is what's important, not the message.

So, if you don't know what the initials HTTP and HTML stand for, not to worry. Use the glossary at the back of this book just to satisfy your curiosity, not because it will help you communicate. Let the technicians have their own turf. They're no threat to true marketers. The term-throwers aren't as sales-driven as marketers are or they wouldn't be term-throwers.

No, the key to understanding the technique of copywriting for the Internet isn't knowing a batch of terms. It's the First Netwriting Rule:

### Stop the surfer in his/her tracks.

Not only is this the first rule, it's the most crucial rule. We'll tell you why—and the reason is true of any new technological development: The typical surfer is Generation-X, male, and totally computer-oriented. In fact, many who are excluded from our brave new world not only have never had any contact with the Internet . . . they have no desire. Here we have a couple of generations of people who can't program their VCRs, and we're asking them to punch in "http://www." and a bunch of letters. To do that, they have to subscribe to an online service or a Web server, have a modem that operates at 28,800 baud, and be interested.

The respected magazine *Adweek* did its own survey in the teeth of massive Internet hype. This survey indicated that penetration was low. Just 20 percent answered "Yes" when asked if they wanted to surf the Internet. As expected, twice as many men answered "Yes" as women.

One more: In late 1995 an *Advertising Age* survey showed that although more than 80 percent of adults had "heard of" the Internet, fewer than half had heard of the World Wide Web. The magazine reported that the biggest group of users was the 18-to-24 age group; next was the 25-to-34 age group. Over-35s lagged. Singles were more likely to surf the Web than marrieds. This survey indicated that twice as many men (26 percent) as women had surfed the Web. Fewer than one in four who visited commercial sites had bought anything. No surprises in any of these findings.

Enough surveys . . . at least until some unity can be shown among the various survey results.

## Will the Net Replace Traditional Media . . . Ever?

We have a growing cadre of surfers who spend more time on the Net than they do at their jobs. It parallels television in the 1950s and 1960s. So will the Internet replace television, radio, newspapers, direct mail, and skywriting? That isn't likely during its explosive first growth, for a whole bunch of reasons we'll explore as we go. Mass it ain't. Class? The jury not only is still out, the jury hasn't been selected yet.

One member of the jury, the Direct Marketing Association, projects that by the year 2004 more than $28 billion of goods and services will be sold by interactive media. Many regard this as ultraconservative because interactive includes not just the Internet but CD-ROM and interactive television. Another estimate that has appeared in print projects $45 billion in goods and services sold via the Internet by the year 2005.

## TOO MUCH HYPE? YES. A BIG FUTURE? YES

We have an advantage today. We're truly in on the ground floor of the most amazing medium of communications since the Tower of Babel toppled. We have to be careful, though, to position the medium properly.

So far, much of the interest is hype. That's bad. So far, much of the copy stinks. That's bad. Both those situations are bad because they'll keep people off the Net. It parallels the fellow who says, "My grandfather once tried direct mail and it didn't work, so why should I send out a mailing?"

## BUT WHO ARE THEY AND WHERE ARE THEY?

We hope everyone agrees that the reason surveys disagree so dramatically is because as the Internet converts itself from a giant embryo to an overfed youngster to a strapping adolescent, the character of those who know it and love it changes, both among marketers and among surfers.

Who are they?

If you're a surfer and your access is through CompuServe, your online name might be 71213.25065@compuserve.com. Who? Privacy pervades the Net as it does no other medium. One reason for the medium's popularity is surfer anonymity.

So name-collection has to be more sophisticated than just an electronic capture. It has to be more sophisticated than asking, "Who are you?"

The technique of name-collecting is obvious to marketers who really want to milk surfer names:

### Reward

Chapters six and eight describe various types of rewards and the most effective ways of presenting them . . . effectiveness being an often-elusive amalgam of *selectivity* (getting the right surfers to ask for the reward) and *titillation* (generating anticipation which brings a payoff).

Let's assume a site has the capability of capturing the names of those who "hit" the site. Not many do, and not many see the value of collecting hit-names. We'll discuss that as we go, but immediately an iconoclastic question presents itself: Of what value is measurement of raw hits who do nothing but land and then move on, unless we can discover who has landed and moved on?

# Hits and Misses

*The Wall Street Journal* reported on the *HotWired* Web site, a Generation-X favorite. *HotWired* counted 600,000 hits a day; but that total represented only about 6,000 surfers.

Similarly, *Penthouse* claimed an astounding two million hits. Those hits, the magazine said, represented 100,000 visits.

How can 100,000 visits mean two million hits? Easy. Each time a surfer moves to a different page, a new hit is counted. So if the average surfer touches 20 pages, 100,000 surfers mean two million hits.

Hits count files, not people. A single mouse-click can translate itself into a dozen hits. Ecstasy over the number of hits bears a disturbingly familiar resemblance to ecstasy over the number of people who "note" an ad or "recall" a commercial. The relationship with actual business transacted is murky.

And wait another moment: Who says the 100,000 surfers are 100,000 different surfers? It could be 20,000 surfers, each making multiple visits.

The astute marketer says, "So what? If we're attracting fewer surfers, but those surfers are showing this kind of loyalty, we're better off than those who get a multitude of meaningless one-time hits."

If all this confuses you, be of good cheer: The medium is implicitly confusing because it still is evolving.

That's why your timing, showing an interest in using the Internet as a marketing medium, is good. If you wait until the dust settles, some of the golden nuggets in that dust will have been claimed before you got there.

**FIGURE 3–1A**

*The Ore-Ida home page successfully serves several different marketing functions, providing
information about both products and company, and also serving a recruitment function.
The three don't conflict, as each points to a different group of internal pages.*

# Welcome To Ore-Ida!

P.O. Box 10
Boise, Idaho
83707
(208)383-6100

### Ore-Ida Family of Products

- Retail Potato and Onion Products
- Retail Specialty Products
- FoodService

### Ore-Ida Facts

- Ore-Ida History

### Ore-Ida Career Opportunities

- About Employment At Ore-Ida Foods

To be notified of anything new or different on the
Ore-Ida Home Page join the Ore-Ida *CyberSpud
Club*.

*Designed to be viewed best with Netscape Browser 1.12 or above.*

**If you have any questions or comments please send them to the Ore-Ida Webmaster at webmaster@oreida.com**
*Copyright © 1995-1996 Ore-Ida Foods, Inc., all rights reserved*
*Last Modified January 19, 1996*

**FIGURE 3–1B**

*An internal page on Ore-Ida's Web site can serve as a home page in its own right, so long as cross-promotion in other media point directly to it. Its URL (http://www. oreida.com.tater-tots/) is reasonable for direct entry into a browser, and the page itself makes sense as a home page (although the unnecessarily detailed photograph downloads slowly enough to discourage surfers from visiting the site).*

**More Than Just Potatoes**

**Recipes of the Month!**

**Sneak Previews of Upcoming Features**

*Designed to be viewed best with Netscape Browser 1.12 or above.*

**If you have any questions or comments please send them to the** <u>Ore-Ida Webmaster</u> at webmaster@oreida.com
*Copyright © 1995-1996 Ore-Ida Foods, Inc., all rights reserved*
*Last Modified February 15, 1996*

## FIGURE 3-2

*American Sales Industries sells premiums and incentives—a product line with a well-defined vertical market. Its home page will simultaneously attract that market and repel casual surfers. In an era of targeted marketing and one-on-one selling, the Web complements other marketing media perfectly.*

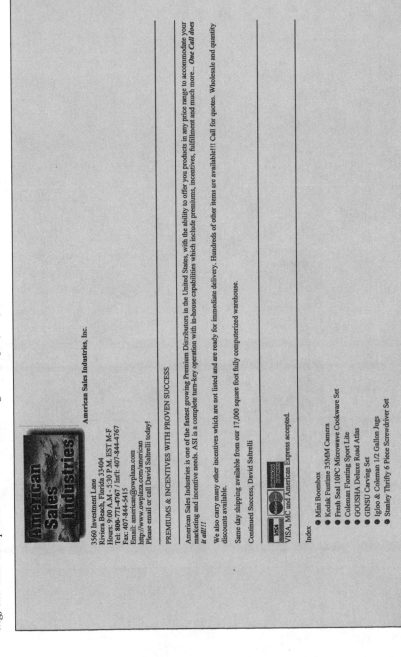

**American Sales Industries, Inc.**

3560 Investment Lane
Riviera Beach, Florida 33404
Hours: 9:00 A.M - 5:30 P.M. EST M-F
Tel: **800-771-4767** / Int'l: 407-844-4767
Fax: 407-844-5415
Email: american@owplaza.com
http://www.owplaza.com/american
Please email or call David Saltrelli today!

PREMIUMS & INCENTIVES WITH PROVEN SUCCESS

American Sales Industries is one of the fastest growing Premium Distributors in the United States, with the ability to offer you products in any price range to accommodate your marketing and incentive needs. ASI is a complete turn-key operation with in-house capabilities which include premiums, incentives, fulfillment and much more... *One Call does it all!!!*

We also carry many other incentives which are not listed and are ready for immediate delivery. Hundreds of other items are available!!! Call for quotes. Wholesale and quantity discounts available.

Same day shipping available from our 17,000 square foot fully computerized warehouse.

Continued Success, David Saltrelli

VISA, MC and American Express accepted.

Index

- Mini Boombox
- Kodak Funtime 35MM Camera
- Fresh Seal 10PC Microwave Cookware Set
- Coleman Floating Sport Lite
- GOUSHA Deluxe Road Atlas
- GINSU Carving Set
- Igloo & Coleman 1/2 Gallon Jugs
- Stanley Thrifty 6 Piece Screwdriver Set

## FIGURE 3–3

*The Beverly Hills Camera Shop looks a lot like a billboard, using similar techniques to immediately grab the attention of camera enthusiasts who happen to be surfing by, or who visit the site because of a cross-promotion but don't know for sure if this is a site that will interest them. The giant "Leica" is a grabber for this crowd, even though it may hold no interest for other constituencies.*

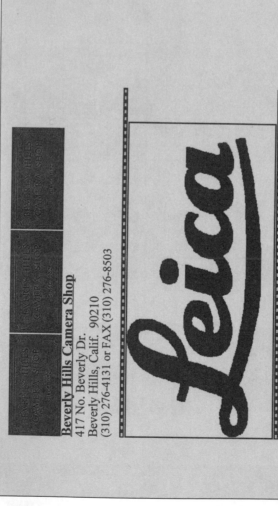

### Beverly Hills Camera Shop
417 No. Beverly Dr.
Beverly Hills, Calif.  90210
(310) 276-4131 or FAX (310) 276-8503

*Leica Specialists* over 60 years.
The Beverly Hills Camera shop was *ESTABLISHED* in 1932 and has been serving the community at the same location since. We carry all major makes of Cameras and accessories.

### Our Speciality is Collectable Cameras and Photographic Equipment

We are dealers for: *Leica,* Nikon, Pentax, Minolta, Minox, Canon, Fuji, Kodak, Yashica, Rollei, Olympus, Polaroid,  and many others.

We handle accessories from: Saunders, Dot-Line, D&F Albums, Webway, Holson, HP Marketing, Satter, PhotoCo, etc.

Feel free to contact me, John Sibley (president – Elite Images, Inc.) anytime. I will be glad to answer any questions you may have.

# 4 Making Yourself Easy to Find

A few absolute words about cross-promoting your Web site:

**You absolutely have to cross-promote your web site.**

In *Field of Dreams,* Kevin Costner's character heard a voice whisper, "If you build it, they will come." He built it, they came. Two differences between *Field of Dreams* and your Web site:

- In *Field of Dreams,* Costner built a baseball field in a cornfield. You're building an electronic needle in a multigigabyte haystack.

- *Field of Dreams* was a movie. You're spending real money on virtual reality.

The Web stands unique among promotional media. Your potential customers have no easy way to know how to find you. Even if you have a reasonable vanity URL, your customers have no easy way of knowing to look in *http://www.abc.com* and not *http://www.abccorp.com* or *http://www.abcinc.com*. And that's assuming they *want* to look for you.

As things now stand, surfers don't have a simple way to browse. There's no window shopping on the Internet. As a general rule, the only people who land on your home page are the ones who came looking for you.

Here's one reason advertisers (as opposed to marketers) can get confused about the Internet. Advertisers use media in which they act as *sponsors*. Somebody else attracts their customers to the media, whether they're advertising on the Superbowl, placing a double-truck ad in a newspaper, sending a classified ad to *Popular Mechanics*, or running a full-page four-color ad in *National Geographic*. For advertisers, somebody else brings them in. Newspaper and magazine editors attract readers with articles of interest to their readers. TV program gurus do the same with programs to win viewer interest. *Then* they see the advertising.

On the other hand, direct marketers create promotional material that has to appeal to potential customers strictly on its own merits, whether it's an infomercial, a direct mail letter, a telemarketing campaign, or a catalog. To direct marketers, creating messages for the Web feels natural. Going for the jugular with one stroke is what they do regularly. But their discipline isn't parallel to Internet marketing either.

Why? Most direct marketing media *intrude* on potential customers. Direct mail and catalogs arrive unsolicited in the mailbox. Telemarketing arrives unbidden over the telephone.

Infomercials have a lot in common with the Web, and in fact the term "surfing the Web" comes from the earlier television term "channel surfing." But infomercials have a different dynamic: Cross-promotions seem to harm viewership, presumably because viewers don't want to admit to themselves that they find infomercials entertaining.

Web surfers have no such inhibition. They're either searching for entertainment or they're specifically looking for you.

Make their job easy. How?

# Register Your Site with the Major Web Indexes

Remember that only beginning surfers, stumbling blindly through the Net, ever visit a site by accident. One way the surfer finds you is by looking for you, or for somebody like you. Services like Yahoo!, Lycos, and InfoSeek provide the Web's table of contents and index. They want you to register with them; you want to register with them. Surfers visit them regularly to find sites of particular interest. Figure 1–1A shows the Yahoo! table of contents. Figure 1–1B shows the results of a Yahoo! search.

Make sure Yahoo! and its major competitors include you in their listings.

## MAKE SURE YOU HAVE THE RIGHT KEYWORDS

Many of the Web directory services use computer programs to automatically wander through the Web, cataloging everything they encounter. You don't have to register with these services. But you do need to make sure your Web site includes every word a potential customer may use to find you. Make a list of key words and check the text of your site to make sure each one appears somewhere.

# Quid Pro Quo: Cross-Postings

Some businesses will be naturals for a mutual assistance pact. They don't compete with you. You don't compete with them. And you can identify some reasonable logic for mutual referrals.

How does it work? The whole point of a "hypertext link" is clicking on highlighted text or a graphical symbol that refers to some other page on the Web—and, by clicking, going there.

Note, please: don't worry about not knowing the mechanics or electronics of hypertext links. A hypertext link doesn't have any restrictions as to whether it refers to a page on the same Web site or to a different one; all sites are equals in the eyes of a hypertext link. Click—you've moved there.

MCI has extended the idea of a cross-posting into a service—marketplaceMCI (Figure 4–1)—which provides a home to a wide variety of merchants. Because MCI also provides Web services, this becomes both more and less than a Web directory service.

It's more because MCI promotes its site to attract customers, just as a shopping mall in the real world promotes itself to the benefits of its merchants. It's less than a directory because Web surfers know MCI's merchants will also appear on the other directories, but the reverse isn't true.

Figure 4–2 shows another ingenious example of cross-postings. The public relations firm Metzger Associates publishes a tongue-in-cheek soap opera called *As the Web Turns*. Updated on a regular basis to attract repeat visitors, each episode includes links to Metzger's clients. Figure 4–2A shows Metzger's home page, Figure 4–2B shows a list of episodes, and Figure 4–2C shows the first episode. Note the highlighted text *Denver Center for the Performing Arts*. Click on it and you go straight to the Denver Center for the Performing Arts home page (Figure 4–2D).

Take advantage of hypertext. Movie theatres can provide links to studios' movie pages in addition to providing schedules, and the studios can provide links back to the theatre schedules. On-line catalogs and their suppliers should cross-reference each other. There's a rich, largely unexplored territory here based on the Web, equivalent to co-op advertising.

But don't take this off a cliff. You want to sell *your* product, not provide your own guide to the World Wide Web. Yahoo!, Alta Vista, Spry, all do a fine job of providing Web guides. You should cross-post judiciously, sparingly, and mutually.

Otherwise you run a peculiar risk. A surfer will enter a generic name, looking for a *category*. You're in there . . . but so are your competitors. Writing in *Catalog Age* in early 1995, Laurie Petersen pointed out that even that early in the game—and the number of sites increases monthly, weekly, daily, hourly, at warp speed—entering "clothing" in Yahoo! yielded 71 matches.

Had she entered *your* site name, she'd have had *one* match.

# GET YOURSELF MENTIONED

The most effective ways of attracting visitors to your Web site aren't part of the Web. Get yourself mentioned.

If your site has some entertainment value (which is what the hot lists look for), use old-fashioned public relations techniques to bring your site to the attention of the publications your customers read. Surfers, always on the lookout for sites more interesting than the usual boring fare they encounter, will flock to any site that promises to keep them entertained.

For example, many magazines now publish lists of hot sites in each issue. Get your site listed.

This underscores the marriage between the creative and the technical. For a publication to recognize your site as *hot,* you'd better heat it up. That's another reason *edutainment* has become an effective Web staple.

Some of the on-line services sponsor an electronic version of scavenger hunts. If the opportunity presents itself, participate. These contests bring people to your site, people who otherwise would never even hear of you. It can be a mixed bag because some of these visitors are in it only for the game and the prizes. If your home page is a spectacular stopping-place, some of them will be back.

Here's a good place to re-emphasize an obvious but often forgotten point: be discriminating about where you publicize your site. Match publicity to your desired targets.

If you're a mass marketer concerned with image, by all means publicize your site everywhere. You're measuring success by the number of hits, not the number of sales your Web site drives. If, in contrast, you have a way to identify your most likely customers, tailor your publicity to the media appealing to those prospects.

Example: If you sell telephone systems, get on the *Computer Telephony Magazine* hot list. If you're an advertising agency, make sure *Advertising Age* has you in its list of sites. If the magazines that cater to your particular market segment don't have a hot list, call the editor and suggest they add one. This medium is new enough that editors take suggestions regarding it with unusual seriousness.

All the major computer trade publications publish hot lists; and because their readership includes a high percentage of Web surfers, they tend to list sites based on the "cool factor," not because of any relationship a site has to the computer industry. If you understand the terminology, a hot site being cool isn't at all remarkable. It's only lingo, but the lingo refers to the preponderance of surfers.

Again, don't be bashful. Shyness and salesmanship just don't go together. Find out who at your local newspaper has an interest in the Web and encourage him or her to write a feature about local businesses that use the Web in innovative ways—you, for example.

For that matter, a growing number of local newspapers have established Web sites, and they all include links to other useful home pages. Typical is *The Star Tribune* in Minneapolis, which has links to movie listings, restaurants, and other local sites of interest. Make sure logical media know about you.

# Promote Your Web Site Everywhere

Your loyal customers will *want* to visit your Web site. Make it easy for them.

Put your URL on all your business cards, right next to your e-mail address. You do have your e-mail address on your business cards, don't you?

Put it on your stationery. You may choose to include it in the letterhead or you might decide to put it at the bottom, which makes it stand out a bit more.

Every print ad you run should include your Web site. @dVenture, "The Electronic Advertising Network," understands this point (Figure 4–3). Like newspapers that understand the need for television, as well as in-paper advertising for the newspaper itself, so @dVenture knows it has to lure people into its Web media-buying service through other media—an expression of strength, not weakness, in its product.

Companies with technical products tend to lead the way here. Note the well-placed but unemphasized URL in Linotype-Hell's print advertisement for its SAPHIR scanner (Figure 4–4). It's there . . . in the last sentence of the ad where readers who skip the rest of the text will probably see it. The value to Linotype-Hell? It can provide lots more information about this highly complex product than it wants to put in a print ad. And logical customers for a product like this will want all the information they can get.

If you're brave, also include your URL in any television advertising. Superimpose it in the last several cuts. Heck, put it on your billboards if you have room.

Obviously, the simpler your site name, the more mnemonic it can be. But the way to look at it, even if you're stuck with a hard-to-remember site name, is: It can't hurt. No exposure hurts. And an unexploited site loses traffic it should have.

Make use of your Web site in direct marketing promotions. In a mailing, direct readers to your Web site for more information, contest hints, special discounts, or as an alternative to your toll-free number and (perhaps toll-free) fax number for placing an order.

A marketing proposal you may find startling until you've tried it: You absolutely *must* offer a discount for people who order through the Web, for two reasons:

1.  Visitors to your Web site aren't dumb.

2.  Visitors to your Web site aren't dumb.

To elaborate: When somebody places an order on your Web site, your transaction costs drop to almost zilch. Every Web shopper not only knows it, but the knowledge generates resentment if some sort of reciprocal compensation doesn't exist. You're saving money. Pass some of it along. That covers point #1.

To explain the second point, recognize that people who visit your site do so on their nickel, not yours. Since they're bearing the expense, give them an incentive—a special discount, or, failing that, lower shipping and handling charges, or something else of perceived value.

Elsewhere in this text we suggest additional incentives, none of which is costly and all of which should produce sales.

## POSITION YOUR SITE WHEN YOU PROMOTE IT

If you just mention your site in your other promotional efforts, you'll draw more visitors than if you don't mention it. If you explain *why* someone should visit your site you'll draw far more.

Experienced marketers recognize this as nothing more than one of the basic rules of marketing—stress *benefit* every chance you get.

This is especially true of Web-based businesses, such as Media Central (Figure 4–5). Media Central doesn't depend on surfers encountering it by accident. It takes its message to the places its potential customers live now.

Web Digest For Marketers (WDFM—Figure 4–6) follows the same strategy, marketing its on-line business in the print media its logical customers read on a regular basis. WDFM stresses benefit throughout its print ad, doing everything it can to lure readers to its site.

A happy by-product of telling surfers why they should land on your site is internal rather than external. You have to tell *yourself* why a surfer should land on your site. If the text and illustrations and sound and demonstrations are flat and dull and unfocused, you'll see the problems in time to strengthen them before unleashing them on outsiders.

Include your URL in a print ad. Discreetly put *http://www.abc.com* in the lower right corner of your ad. Readers who see your Net address may make note of it and visit your site the next time it occurs to them. You can bet it won't happen if you don't publicize your site.

If you say *For complete technical specifications about this and all of our other products, visit our Web site at http://www.abc.com,* you'll draw a far greater percentage of readers to your site.

If you become known for special Web site offers, you'll bring them back to you again and again.

Don't stop there!

Always . . . *always* . . . ALWAYS . . . **ALWAYS** . . . exploit the interactivity of the medium. Even if you're only using the Web for image advertising and have no interest in selling directly or indirectly, you can give visitors a way to communicate with you, helping cement their relationship with you.

Go beyond this tentative step. Do something to capture the identity, interests, demographics, and psychographics of every visitor to your site. Hold a contest, offer free coupons, free software, your electronic newsletter—and make it easy. Living down a reputation for having a dull, obfuscatory, or difficult site can take years. On your site, all a visitor has to do is to fill out a small on-screen form.

At the very least, interactivity can be as simple as a push button labeled, "Send me more information" or "Have a sales representative call me." Another push button is labeled, "I'd like to be told about new products," and another that says, "Please send me your complete catalog."

Cross-promoted Web sites may be the ultimate generator of highly qualified sales leads. Take advantage of the opportunity.

And, of course, give every shopper the chance to buy. Put an order form on their computer screen, along with your toll-free phone number and fax-in ordering number.

You're in business to do business, using the most dynamic and exciting medium yet devised. Take advantage of it.

**FIGURE 4–1A**

*marketplaceMCI, an electronic mall, exists to promote other businesses on the Web, just as real shopping malls promote the merchants inside.*

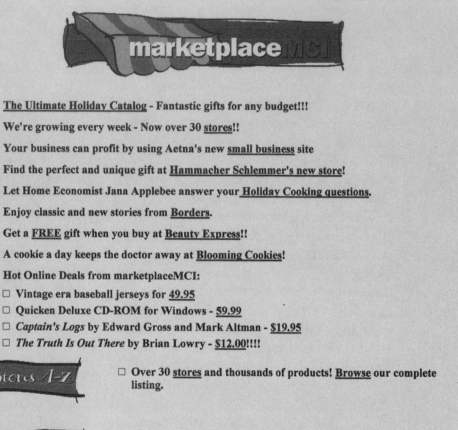

- The Ultimate Holiday Catalog - Fantastic gifts for any budget!!!
- We're growing every week - Now over 30 stores!!
- Your business can profit by using Aetna's new small business site
- Find the perfect and unique gift at Hammacher Schlemmer's new store!
- Let Home Economist Jana Applebee answer your Holiday Cooking questions.
- Enjoy classic and new stories from Borders.
- Get a FREE gift when you buy at Beauty Express!!
- A cookie a day keeps the doctor away at Blooming Cookies!
- Hot Online Deals from marketplaceMCI:
  - ☐ Vintage era baseball jerseys for 49.95
  - ☐ Quicken Deluxe CD-ROM for Windows - 59.99
  - ☐ *Captain's Logs* by Edward Gross and Mark Altman - $19.95
  - ☐ *The Truth Is Out There* by Brian Lowry - $12.00!!!!

☐ Over 30 stores and thousands of products! Browse our complete listing.

☐ Men's and Women's Designer Fragrances from Beauty Express make great gifts!!.
☐ Great Floral Arrangements from FTD Online!!

☐ Hundreds of ideas
☐ Flowers for someone you love ... or just like!

☐ Software for Windows and Mac
☐ Great hardware at great prices
☐ News and views about computers

**FIGURE 4-1B**

- [ ] **Insurance, news & tips at Aetna's new <u>small Business</u> site**
- [ ] **<u>Office supplies</u> for every size of business**
- [ ] **<u>MCI PrePaid Calling Card</u> - There are no more excuses for not calling**
- [ ] **<u>Vital business</u> information**

**<u>Secure Purchasing</u> at marketplaceMCI**

## Need help?

- [ ] A note on security and shopping for users of <u>AOL and Prodigy</u>
- [ ] New to shopping on the net? Click <u>here</u> for more information.
- [ ] Interested in getting your own store on the net? Click <u>here</u> to learn more.

| InternetMCI | marketplaceMCI | Shopping Basket | Feedback | Holiday Catalog |

**FIGURE 4–2A**

*Metzger Associates, a public relations firm, created a serialized campy soap opera on its site, called* As the Web Turns. *At least for those visitors who enjoy the style, new episodes provide a motivator for repeat visits on a regular basis. But this is* not *the principal reason behind this unusual device.*

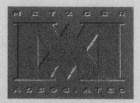

Welcome to the <u>Metzger Associates</u> home page. We're a Boulder, Colorado PR firm providing media relations, writing services, investor relations and online communications for clients across the country.

<u>As the Web Turns</u>, our on-line weekly soap opera, is offered by Metzger Associates' creative staff solely for the entertainment of visitors to our home page.

For material information on publicly held companies, <u>EDGAR</u>, which lists SEC filings on companies that file electronically.

To visit Web sites of publicly held companies, see our <u>List of Public Companies</u>.

For other financial information on the WWW, including the MIT experimental stock price server, foreign exchanges, stock market newsletters and even a few stock market games, visit the <u>National Corporate Services</u> home page.

Visit the <u>Rockies Venture Club Information Center</u>. The RVC is the premier venture capital club in the Rocky Mountain region.

The Colorado Chapter of the <u>Public Relations Society of America</u> has established its web presence to help members and non-members alike learn about PR and PRSA activities.

**The following is a list of our online clients:**

<u>*The Boulder Technology Incubator*</u> is one of the nation's first technology business incubators. BTI provides capital sourcing, economic facilities and support services to its high-tech start-up residents.

**CASE LOGIC** <u>*Case Logic*</u> is an industry leader in music storage products and computer accessories.

DCC <u>*Dependent Care Connection*</u> is a national leader in providing counseling, education and referral services to more than 95 corporate clients representing more than 600,000 covered lives.

**imex** <u>*Imex Medical Systems*</u> manufactures cardiovascular diagnostic equipment and is a

**FIGURE 4–2B**

*As Metzger Associates creates new episodes of its on-line soap opera, it adds them to the table of contents for easy reference.*

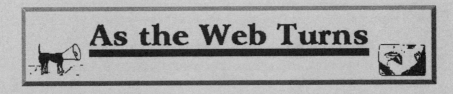

Episode One - After the Opera

Episode Two - At Pinecliffe General

Episode Three - Birds of Prey

Episode Four - A Double-Edged Sword

Episode Five - A CD Affair

Episode Six - The Grassy Knolls of the Mind

Episode Seven - Les Fleurs du Mal

Episode Eight - The Unbearable Lightness of Being Gaelic

Episode Nine - A Black Brew

Episode Ten - Angels of Mercy

Episode Eleven - Country on My Mind

Episode Twelve - Pitching a Tent On the Cholesterol Superhighway

Episode Thirteen - Smoke Gets In Your Eyes

Episode Fourteen - Dance of Death

Episode Fifteen - Bring on the Hounds

Episode Sixteen - Leap of Faith

Episode Seventeen - Homeward Bound

Episode Eighteen - Falling from Grace

Episode Nineteen - Some Enchanted Evening

Episode Twenty - I'm Gonna Get You, Sucka'

**FIGURE 4–2C**

*An episode of Metzger Associates* As the Web Turns, *showing a hypertext link to a client Web site: the Denver Center for the Performing Arts, a Metzger client. The rationale behind the "Soap Opera" comes clear.*

**As the Web Turns**

Cast of Characters

Episode One

**After the Opera**

Rosalia sat behind the wheel of her red BMW 320i in the parking lot of the Denver Center for the Performing Arts. Bizet's Carmen was as stirring as ever, Preston thought as he sat beside her. At a time, it probably made as much commotion as Rosalia did tonight in her daring red velvet evening dress. She was fiery, alright. She wore red and only red. But even the passion she wore it with every day could never exhaust the fire that burned inside her.

Preston was drawn to this flame like a moth. He lingered perilously close to a force that drew him to the edge of a void -- a void containing very little, except the fiery infernos of the eternally damned. He steadied himself, remembering what brought him to this dangerous place.

Rosalia turned away, leaning against the exit chute of the car's side-impact airbag. It made her feel safe and secure, the way Preston made her feel. She had never met a man like him before. He was like half a mythical creature walking on four cloven hooves, half the title character of an unnamed chapter of a never-published book called "An Illustrated History of Math Nerds."

Preston had asked her the most dangerous of questions. She knew there could be only one response.

End of Episode One

Go to the Next Episode

Go to the Latest Episode

*Concept: Bret Clement*
*Story: (c) Lance Jones*
*Illustration: Sherrie Lotito*

**FIGURE 4–2D**

*The Denver Scientific and Cultural Facilities District home page, reached from the hypertext link, is embedded in* As the Web Turns.

# Scientific and Cultural Facilities District

Established in 1988 by the voters in metropolitan Denver, the SCFD distributes funds generated by a sales tax equalling one penny on a $10 purchase to support scientific and cultural facilities within the six metro counties: Adams, Arapahoe, Boulder, Denver, Douglas and Jefferson. More than 200 non-profit arts and science organizations have received funding from the District, supporting hundreds of programs and events that have reached millions of people.

Who Receives SCFD Funds?
The SCFD: Why and How?
SCFD Free Days
Feedback: Tell the SCFD How to Better Serve You

## Who Receives SCFD Funds?

Nearly every arts or cultural organization in the Denver metropolitan area is eligible to receive SCFD funding. Qualifying organizations must have been in operation for at least two years and must be involved in arts or culture as their primary purpose.

The SCFD currently provides support to more than 200 organizations, ranging from large institutions like the Denver Museum of Natural History to smaller theaters, arts councils and dance groups. SCFD recipient organizations are grouped by size into three levels of funding:

**Tier I**

Denver Art Museum
Denver Botanic Gardens
Denver Museum of Natural History
Denver Zoo

**Tier II** - (Organizations with annual operating incomes of more than $700,000)

Arvada Center for the Arts & Humanities
Central City Opera
Cherry Creek Arts Festival
Children's Museum
Cleo Parker Robinson Dance
Colorado Ballet
Colorado Music Festival

**FIGURE 4–3**

*@dVenture, the Electronic Advertising Network, is a media buyer for the World Wide Web. It understands the need to promote itself in other media, rather than waiting for business to find it on the Web. This advertisement ran in a trade magazine.*

**FIGURE 4–4**
*This print ad for the SAPHIR scanner from Linotype-Hell demonstrates both cross-promotion of its Web site (note the last sentence of ad copy) and excellent use of the Web to provide technical information to prospective customers. In this case, potential buyers will probably want a lot more information than Linotype-Hell would want to squeeze into a space ad. Synergy between other media and the Web is another "sleeping giant" the Web can claim as a legitimate offspring.*

**Some people scan in RGB**

**Some people scan in CMYK**

**Maybe you should see what happens
when you scan in CIELAB**

The only way to capture the maximum amount of color data from your original is to scan into the CIELAB color space. And the only way to scan in the CIELAB color space on your desktop is with the new SAPHIR scanner with LinoColor™ software, from the world leader in high-end color scanning: Linotype-Hell.

SAPHIR provides fast one-pass scanning and ColorSync® 2.0 compatibility. LinoColor software provides the most powerful color software ever put into a desktop system. Basically, it gives you the same color capabilities that prepress shops and printers have been using for years. Yet it's so easy to use that even novices can achieve professional-quality results in almost no time at all.

So why limit yourself? Get the full color you deserve. With SAPHIR and LinoColor. Only from Linotype-Hell. For more information, call 800-842-9721. In Canada, 800-668-0770. Or visit us on the Web at http://www.linotype.com

**Linotype-Hell**     CIRCLE (104) ON FREE INFORMATION CARD

© 1995 Linotype-Hell Linotype and Hell are registered trademarks. LinoColor is a trademark of Linotype-Hell AG and/or its subsidiaries. ColorSync is a registered trademark of Apple Computer, Inc.

**FIGURE 4–5**

*Some businesses exist exclusively on the Web itself. Media Central, part of Cowles New Media, is an example. Just because a business runs on the Web doesn't mean all promotion should be on the Web. Media Central markets itself in other media because its likely customers read other media. Hence, this space ad.*

## At last there's a web site just for you and thousands of your marketing and media colleagues.

Announcing **Media Central**, the exciting new Internet web site created exclusively for marketing and media executives like you.

It's your headquarters. Where news is broken, information is gathered, contacts are made. And media and marketing are the only languages spoken.

It's the *in* place. The source. The undisputed authority where you go to check things out — because **Media Central** is the only one-stop online storehouse of the wide-ranging intelligence today's media and marketing pros need to succeed, whether in traditional media or emerging interactive technologies.

Here's what you'll find:
- Daily news briefings covering the hot, fast-breaking stories
- Networking & career resources
- Forums for trading information and finding solutions
- Discussions with media luminaries and trendsetters
- Valuable statistics & surveys
- Central interactive media & marketing resource center
- Valuable web links ... and more!

**Media Central.** It's the home away from home for today's media and marketing professionals. And now that you have the address, you're invited to move in.

Visit *Pre* Online!

Stop by the **Pre** page of Media Central and meet your favorite editors and columnists...and get news and features prepared exclusively for Media Central, which won't appear in the magazine.

COWLES NEW MEDIA
A Division of
Cowles Business Media

**Media Central**
www.mediacentral.com
Your daily source for media & marketing intelligence

**FIGURE 4-6**

WDFM, the Web Digest For Marketers, is another Web-based information business. As with Media Central, WDFM understands the need to market where its customers live. Better than Media Central, WDFM stresses benefit throughout this ad in a direct marketing publication.

# Special offers for Web Marketers at http://advert.com/wdfm/wdfm.html

**Surf over to the WDFM site for high value offers that specially target you, a marketer on the World Wide Web. You'll see offers from American Demographic Magazine, Electronic Newsstand, Riddler, Hotel Discount and many more.**

If you're interested in advertising in this high traffic site, send email to specials@advert.com or call The Online Ad Agency at 212 876-1096. WDFM is a service of the Online Ad Agency.

# 5 Seizing the Netsurfer's Attention

Here's an IQ-test fragment: a list of four items. Three belong together; the fourth does not. See if you can figure out the one that doesn't' fit:

- Watching paint dry
- Watching grass grow
- Watching *I Love Lucy* reruns
- Watching most Web pages load

You've got it! The *I Love Lucy* reruns have a tiny bit of residual attention-getting value.

Why, oh why, so many Web pages cry out for euthanasia is beyond all understanding. And it doesn't have to be that way.

When you put your Web site together, assume you have 5 seconds to grab your prospective customer's attention and hold it.

That's not 5 seconds as measured by the designer of your Web page, sitting at a Power Macintosh and connected directly to your Web server through a high-speed local area network link.

That's 5 seconds as measured by visitors to your site, using a PC with a modem. For every second your designer waits to see a page unfold, your visitors, too many of them connected by slow 14,400 bit-per-second modems, wait about 100 seconds. Quite a difference.

The mechanics of the medium impose constraints as well as offering unique creative advantages. You have to recognize those constraints and work within them, while still designing your site to exploit the Web's strengths . . . which leads to the Four Rules of Web Site Construction:

# Rule No. 1: Never Be the Bottleneck

Rule No. 1 requires no creativity at all. It simply means running your site on a computer powerful enough to handle the load, using a fast-enough connection to the Internet that the bits don't have to wait in line on your end of the network.

All you need is money, and not all that much of it, unless you're so successful that you don't need this book, which means you can afford it anyway.

Why does this rule precede all the others?

Simple: even the most professional creative work will go ignored when potential customers move on, refusing to wait until it appears.

Figures 5–1 and 5–2 show the home pages from two competing banks, Citibank and Chase Manhattan. Somewhat out of key with contemporary financial marketing, both home pages lack specifics. But both did adhere to Rule No. 1 (though they missed Rule No. 3–*Always Have Something New*). Even the bulky graphics downloaded fast enough to require no more than moderate patience, and the text appeared in just two or three seconds.

But neither one considered Rule No. 2.

# Rule No. 2: Put "Grabbers" EARLY in the <u>Text</u>

Text displays before graphics on the Web, and visitors watch the screen s-l-o-w-l-y come into being. Assuming you don't violate Rule No. 1, your text will appear in just a couple of seconds. Put at least one item in it that makes a potential customer wait for that stunning graphic.

How early in the text? Make sure it appears above the scrolling region on your home page. Test this on a computer running the lowest resolution available—640 × 480 pixel resolution on IBM-compatible personal computers. If you have to scroll down to see your grabber, it's too low.

Note how the text in the slow-appearing home page in Figure 5–3 is so generalized that the surfer may not stay to become even a casual visitor:

> Today, your world is more wide open than ever before. The people of U S WEST are exploring the latest advancements in technology and finding ways to turn them into practical solutions that help you live and work on your own terms. Giving you the control, the freedom and the choices you need to interact with your world, your way.

Ignoring the grammatical problem—a last sentence without a subject—we have a communications problem. Verbiage one accepts in an annual report doesn't inspire a site visitor to hang around.

As a guess: Ignoring Rule No. 2 is the most widespread cause of site failure that exists.

Note how the U S WEST presentation violates Rule 2. If, after viewing the uninspiring listing on the home page, you still click on "Products & Services," you move to "Your World, Your Way." There interest heightens with "!nteract"—despite the bland, self-serving description. Click, and you move to "Introducing !nteract," where interest again increases—although the uncommunicative bullet ("The simple answer to business interactions") and the equally ersatz headline aren't great motivators.

Although interest increases as one goes through the multiple pages, many, many surfers won't get that far.

Speaking of simple answers: Be sure your home page graphic repeats the offer . . . and also be sure it fits above the scrolling region (there's no point in having a snazzy graphic your visitors can see only one piece at a time). You have to repeat your grabbers in the graphic because the graphic will push your text down when it appears, and you want to make sure it's always right there in front of every visitor to your site.

Take another look at Kodak's home page in Chapter Two (Figure 2–2). Yes, it has a snappy picture, visible to anyone willing to wait more than half a minute while it loads. Not one item in the text demands that a visitor wait that long.

What constitutes a grabber? That depends on the purpose of your site, and a surprising number of marketers seem to be unsure what that should be.

The litany: You need to tailor your Web site to your marketing strategy. The best models are those outlined in Chapter Two:

1. Customer Service → Stronger Relationship → Customer Retention and Upselling

2. Useful Information → Increased Consumption → More Purchases

3. Convenient Buying + Discounts → Direct Sales + Reduced Overhead

4. New Entertainment Dimension → Increased Product Involvement → Repeat Business

5. Brand Enhancement → Customer Loyalty + Improved Margins

If you're a software company, you probably follow the first model. What's a grabber?

- "Download the latest bug-fixes—FREE."
- "FREE macro library."

- "Contest—FREE computers for the 10 most innovative uses for our products."

- "Suggest a new feature and get a FREE upgrade."

Customers will see these and wait—guaranteed. The word *Free* has retained its magic despite generations of abuse, not only on the Web where too often it's tied to qualifiers, but in every medium of communication.

Figure 5–4A is Novell's home page. Following Novell's long tradition of understated marketing, it lets visitors download a valuable piece of software—Client 32 for Win95—but fails to mention either that the software is valuable, or that it's free. Simply adding the word "FREE" to the beginning of the second December highlight (in Figure 5–4A) would drive response up. Repositioning it so it appears on the first screen—viewers have to scroll down to see it—also would drive up response. Even just moving it up on the page—making it the first bullet in the December listing—would help. In Figure 5–4B you see that Novell continues to *not* emphasize that this software comes at not charge, or that it will benefit the user.

Ragu's Home Page (Figure 2–4) obeys Rule No. 2, and enhances it by offering a contest right on top. Ragu follows the second model admirably. It provides over 150 recipes that use Ragu products, each of which can lead to increased retail sales.

# Rule No. 3: Always Highlight Something New

Well, of course. The Web marketer should value and revere this rule above every other marketing medium. Yes, you can survive with the same old stuff if you're selling consumables to repeat customers. If you're so tired that your customers make you happy by placing the same order every time, you may as well retire now. Aggressive marketers exploit relationships to increase their share of their best customers' business.

A bright and easy example is the Anorak presence, reached through Yahoo!'s "Entertainment" sector (Figure 5–5 A–B). Anorak is a United Kingdom bright light, bringing, as the first option aptly predicts, "bloke-sized chunks of UK tabloid news and sport, prize winning quizzes and intl news photos every day at 10 a.m. UK time."

The combination of guaranteed daily changes and tabloid exposés is irresistible. And, moving through the site, the visitor isn't disappointed because sprightly text moves right along, never becoming overdescriptive and never slowing its pace.

You won't get more of a customer's business without offering the customer something to spend more of his or her money on.

What can you have that's new? Products, for one. Product *uses* for another as the pages for Healthy Choice (Figure 5–6 A–D) show. The company gives a new reason to return to its site every day for a new healthy recipe using—what else?—Healthy Choice products. Providing other health-conscious and healthy-living-oriented sources of information, such as a magazine, also helps. If at all possible at least a third of your products should be new each year. On the Web, that means you can highlight a new product or product use or two each week on your home page.

Is there some information you have that your customers may find useful? If you're a bank, you can show current rates for mortgages, automobile loans, CDs, and savings accounts . . . as they change in real time if you want. (If you want to be more adventurous, accept loan applications on your Web site. If you're even more adventurous, offer complete on-line banking as many of your competitors have started to do.)

Database information is a wonderful source of return visitors. And every time someone comes back, you have another chance to grab him or her with a special offer.

Far more than any other factor, the need for newness catches the unwary off-guard in this medium. It all looks (and is) so simple. Just scan in a bunch of stuff, code some basic HTML, and you're off and running.

Like running, creating and maintaining a successful Web site takes stamina as well as talent.

# Rule No. 4: Offer Interactivity EARLY in the <u>Text</u>

People use their personal computers instead of watching television when they want to interact with a device instead of passively watching it. Give your visitors what they want: a chance to *do* something instead of watching you do it. The positioning rules are the same as those for the grabber—in the text above the scrolling region; repeated in your graphic.

You have no limits in creating opportunities for interaction. A few ideas:

- Games
- Contests
- Prize Drawings
- Animated demonstrations (yes, you can do this)
- Searches and database queries
- 3-dimensional virtual realities your visitors can control (yes, you can do this too)
- Free software downloads
- Requests for customer feedback
- Discussion areas

Figure 5–7 (Lawlinks) uses interactivity to light up what many would anticipate being a dull site, to be visited only *in extremis*. Here we have a difficult objective: being of interest to both attorneys and consumers. Much of the home page is of no interest whatever to consumers . . . nor is it so intended.

But then note the first item in the list of Special Features: the Winning Moves' "Judge 'n' Jury Trial." NOTE THAT TERMINOLOGY: It's "Judge 'n' Jury" not "Judge and Jury." The difference between the two, in perceived complexity and perceived entertainment value, is 180 degrees.

An advertiser in this site, a candidate for judge, presents a standard resumé . . . in key with a "Legal Resource Center" but out of key with the typical Internet visitor.

This "For Circuit Court Judge" insert exemplifies what happens when an advertiser—and that's what this candidate is—ignores the gigantic Internet benefit of interactivity.

## Advertising Agency? Or Marketing Agency?

Before you look at any illustration beyond Figure 5–7, a question: Suppose you ask a marketer for a single positioning sentence. The marketer comes up with: "On the frontal lobe of technology." Would you be eager to continue the conversation?

This is the heading on a Web presence for a major advertising agency. The statement of purpose:

> As a marketing communications team, we're dedicated to the development and implementation of new media and new technologies to enhance *our clients'* ability to deliver an effective marketing message.

Does that statement deliver an effective marketing message? We chose this agency as an example (Figure 5–8), but as Figures 5–9, 5–10, and 5–11 show, advertising agencies lag in their recognition of the Web, not only as the medium most insistent on specifics against tired generalizations but also as the foremost interactive medium.

Interactivity makes the Web unique. Exploit it.

**FIGURE 5–1**

*Any major financial institution walks a tightrope. If copy is aggressive, some will recoil: "A bank should be dignified." If copy is staid, others will recoil: "Yeah, here's a typical stuffed-shirt banker." But the tightrope gets slack on the Web because of the nature and attitude of the typical visitor. If you happened upon this site, would any phrase or graphic on it overcome the quick reaction, "This is going to be dull"? Holding off on specifics— or for that matter, even* one *specific—isn't competitive Web psychology.*

**FIGURE 5-2**

*Asterisks in a Web home page? Please, no. This credit card offer loses steam by delaying distinctive comparisons. A "Want to . . . ?" reference to free airline tickets or dining discounts, even though these benefits would be tied to extra fees and exclusions, would hold the visitor.*

**FIGURE 5–3A**

*Slow download, added to unexciting self-serving information, says to the site visitor: Ho-hum for us and ho-hum for you. This site might have expanded by a thousand percent the size of the tiny "New" icons and included a stimulating hint of whatever the newness represents.*

Today, your world is more wide open than ever before. The people of U S WEST are exploring the latest advancements in technology and finding ways to turn them into practical solutions that help you live and work on your own terms. Giving you the control, the freedom and the choices you need to interact with your world, your way.

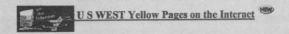 **U S WEST Yellow Pages on the Internet** *NEW*

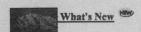 **What's New** *NEW*

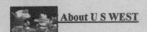 **About U S WEST**

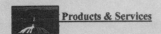 **Products & Services**

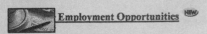 **Employment Opportunities** *NEW*

 **Index**

**Search** the U S WEST Site

**FIGURE 5–3B**

PRODUCTS & SERVICES    U S WEST
Your World. Your Way.

your world. your way.

---

"Your Way" is exploring the possibilites of technology to find practical solutions. By creating products and services, U S WEST gives you the power to interact with your world, your way.

 **!NTERACT**

The Internet-based computer networking service for barrier-free business-to-business communications. Section includes: the new product announcement, an in-depth description, insight and the team.

 **ISDN (Integrated Services Digital Network).**

Simple answers to your questions regarding ISDN. Section includes: Description, Availability, Pricing and How to Order.

 **Your Home Phone.**

Simple answers to your home telecommunication needs. Section includes: What's New on the Horizon, Simple Answers for Residential Needs, Current Special Offers, Residential Products and Services.

 **Your Home Office.**

Simple answers to make your home office run smoother and more efficiently. Section includes: Home Office Products and Services, Consulting Center, Simple Answers for Home Office Needs, and Home Office Resource Guide.

 **Your Small Business.**

**FIGURE 5–3C**

INTRODUCING
!NTERACT.

**The complete
Internet-based computer
networking service . . .
brought to you by
!NTERPRISE
Networking Services
from U S WEST ®
Communications.**

Now there's a simple way
for businesses to meet
global application
networking requirements.
Introducing !NTERACT
(TM), the first complete
and integrated portfolio of
secure applications
services for
business-to-business
communications. . . carried
over secure public lines
and global Internet
connections.

!NTERACT lets
businesses rapidly and
easily share information,
messages, and networked
desktop computer
programs. . . between
colleagues, business
partners, or customers . . .
regardless of where they
are in the world, or the
type of desktop computer
they use.

**FIGURE 5–4A**

*The first December highlight could be exciting, but by emphasizing "we" instead of "you" this Web ad seems to be deliberately unexciting.*

[ <u>Text Only</u> | <u>Feedback</u> | <u>Copyright ©1995 Novell, Inc</u> ]

**December Highlights:**

 **Novell Launches Its Next Generation of <u>TUXEDO: System 6.1</u>**

 **NetWare Clients: <u>Client 32 for Win95</u>, <u>Client for Mac OS v5.1</u>**

**NetWare <u>Web Server</u> Offers a Fast, Easy Web Publishing Solution**

## FIGURE 5–4B
*This page invites the visitor to download Client 32. It's a free offer, but for some reason the company ignores this motivator.*

# Novell NetWare Client 32 for Windows 95 Open Beta

Download Client 32 for Windows 95 | Client 32 Information | Current Issues - FAQ | Submit Problem Report

The NetWare Client 32 for Windows 95 available is dated: October 30, 1995

**Links To Helpful Information**
- Windows 95 Information
- Novell NetWare Client Information - Includes DOS/Windows, OS/2, Macintosh, etc.
- Novell NetWare Utilities / Printing Information
- Search Novells Technical Information Database

Please Email any suggestions for improving this WWW page to clientwww@novell.com
Note: Technical Support Questions will not be responded to

**FIGURE 5–5A**

*Outside the UK, some of the references in this site might be unfamiliar. But no matter. The technique of "inside" name-dropping and hints of naughtiness stop the surfer in his/her tracks.*

YAHOO!

YAHOO INFO — ADD URL — WRITE US

**SHOPPING WITHOUT SCHLEPPING, CLICK HERE.**

## Entertainment:Magazines:Entertainment:Tabloids:Anorak

<u>Options</u>

☐ <u>Anorak</u> - brings you bloke-sized chunks of UK tabloid news and sport, prize winning quizzes and intl news photos every day at 10 am UK time.
☐ Anorak - The Front Pages - latest in UK tabloids

**FIGURE 5–5B**

# ANORAK'S HOMEPAGE AND CONTENTS
The boys who gave the Sex Pistols their inspiration: <u>New York Dolls</u>

\* *<u>Tabloid RoundUp</u>* \* *<u>Anorak Unzipped</u>* \* *<u>Quizzes & Competitions</u>* \* *<u>Text Only Index</u>* \*

**Please resize your screen to the width of the bar above to get the best read out of Anorak**

If you're not using Netscape 1.1 (or higher) you may want to change your browser to Netscape's <u>latest version</u> to ensure that Anorak is displayed as intended.

We would like Anorak to be as "browser friendly" as possible. Please help us to do this by <u>letting us know</u> if you have any difficulty in reading Anorak or have any suggestions on how we could improve the look and speed of our magazine.

"it's not just London... it's not just a Mall"
*when you've finished reading Anorak check out London Mall.*

http://www.anorak.co.uk - email <u>anorak@dial.pipex.com</u> - © 1995 Lightwater Media Ltd. All Rights Reserved.
Reproduction in whole or in part without written permission is strictly prohibited.

**FIGURE 5–6A**

*This marketer does a powerful job of presenting a mundane group of products in a delightfully Web-wise manner. Notice the enticing wording—"Free stuff," not "Free offer." And notice the tie-ins to related information and new ideas for using Healthy Choice products.*

**FIGURE 5–6B**

*"Never say no to a cream sauce."*

WELCOME TO THE KITCHENS OF HEALTHY CHOICE.
WE HAVE VERY STRICT RULES FOR EATING. **EXTRA EVERYTHING.**
CHOW DOWN ON THIS:

- THE COFFEE KLATSCH CHAT. Talk about food, recipes and share information on healthy eating.
- THIS MONTH'S RECIPE MAKEOVER
- RAID THE FRIDGE. Ice cream, dinners, entrees, cheese and meats.
- OPEN THE CUPBOARD. Pasta sauces, ketchup, soup, cereal and popcorn.
- THE MENU PLANNER. A complete 7 day menu plan for healthy eating.
- THE RECIPE BOX
- COOKING CLASS. Cooking tips from the Healthy Choice chefs.
- THE HEALTHY CHOICE NUTRITIONIST
- "OUR FAVORITE LINKS"

**FIGURE 5–6C**

## A Healthy Choice Weekly Menu
*Quote from the Nutritionist-*
*"Eating well means eating what you love. Healthy Choice has it all."*

| MENU DAY 1 | | Nutrition Information | |
|---|---|---|---|
| **BREAKFAST** | 1 slice banana bread with:<br>    2 ounces <u>Healthy Choice Smoked Chicken Breast</u><br>    1 teaspoon soft margerine<br>1/2 cup strawberries<br>Coffee | Calories | 1858 |
| | | Protein | 103 g |
| | | Carbohydrate | 267 g |
| **LUNCH** | 2 quesadillas, each made by melting:<br>    1 ounce <u>Healthy Choice Fat Free Mexican Cheese Shreds</u> inside:<br>    1 folded flour tortilla<br>Rice and Beans simmered to yield:<br>    1/2 cup kidney beans (canned, rinsed)<br>    1/2 cup cooked rice<br>    1/4 cup chopped tomato<br>    2 tablespoons mince onion<br>1/2 sliced mango<br>Sparkling water | Fat | 49 g |
| | | Saturated Fat | 9 g |
| | | Cholesterol | 44 mg |
| | | Calcium | 1312 mg |
| | | Iron | 16 mg |
| | | Sodium | 2359 mg |
| | | Vitamin A | 5522 RE |
| **DINNER** | <u>Healthy Choice Chicken Fettucini Entree</u><br>3/4 cup carrots with mint and orange juice<br>1/2 cup sliced tomato on lettuce:<br>    1 tablespoon balsamic vinegar<br>1 slice Italian bread with:<br>    1 teaspoon olive oil<br>1 cup skim milk | Vitamin C | 146 mg |
| | | % Calories from Fat | 23% |
| | | % Calories from Saturated Fat | 6% |
| **SNACKS** | 1 serving <u>Rainbow Dessert Pizza</u> (see recipe)<br>1/3 cup unsalted peanuts | To boost the calorie level to 2,100 to 2,300 calories, add: 1/4 sliced mango (lunch), 1 slice Italian bread with 1 teaspoon olive oil (dinner), 1/2 cup pineapple sorbet (dinner) | |

| MENU DAY 2 | | Nutrition Information | |
|---|---|---|---|
| **BREAKFAST** | 1 ounce honey bran cereal topped with:<br>    3/4 cup low-fat fruit yogurt<br>    3 tablespoons unsalted sunflower seeds<br>3/4 cup apricot nectar | Calories | 1830 |
| | | Protein | 77 g |
| | | Carbohydrate | 309 g |
| | | Fat | 38 g |
| **LUNCH** | 1 serving <u>Two-Bean Chili Franks</u> (see recipe)<br>1/2 cup raw zucchini sticks<br>1/2 cup sliced apple<br>1 cup skim milk<br>1/2 cup <u>Healthy Choice Praline and Caramel Premium Low Fat Ice Cream</u><br>Sparkling water | Saturated Fat | 8 g |
| | | Cholesterol | 98 mg |
| | | Calcium | 917 mg |
| | | Iron | 16 mg |
| | | Sodium | 2193 mg |
| **DINNER** | <u>Healthy Choice Beef Sirloin Tips Dinner</u><br>1/2 cup sliced tomato on lettuce leaf with:<br>    1 tablespoon red wine vinegar<br>1 cinnamon roll<br>1 cup skim milk | Vitamin A | 1671 RE |
| | | Vitamin C | 184 mg |
| | | % Calories from Fat | 18% |
| | | % Calories from Saturated Fat | 4% |
| **SNACKS** | 1 1/2 slices banana bread<br>2 tablespoons <u>Healthy Choice Fat Free Plain Cream Cheese</u> (soft)<br>1 pear | To boost the calorie level to 2,100 to 2,300 calories, add: 2 homemade chocolate chip cookies (lunch), 1 cinnamon roll (dinner), 1/2 slice banana bread (snack), 1 tablespoon <u>Healthy Choice Plain Fat Free Cream Cheese</u> (snack) | |

| MENU DAY 3 | | Nutrition Information | |
|---|---|---|---|

**FIGURE 5–7A**

*Inclusion of interactive elements and, especially, the apparently minor reduction of "Judge and Jury Trial" to the more convivial "Judge 'n' Jury Trial," help this site's affability. The ad by a circuit court judge candidate misses completely the nature of Internet uniqueness.*

---

Home Page ❖ Attorney Center ❖ Consumer Center ❖ Law Mall ❖ email

## LawLinks
### The Internet Legal Resource Center

**Welcome to the Internet's most comprehensive legal resource site for both Attorneys and Consumers.**

You Are Visitor #
**40793**
Join LawLinks User List

### FREE Attorney Home Page Offer!
Special Offer to Bar Associations

*We are proud to have been named "Best Law Related Site" in the October issue of* THE STICK *Websurfer Newsletter!*

| Attorney Center | | Consumer Center |
|---|---|---|
| Legal Software Reviews | Attorney Home Pages | Consumer Mall |
| Computer Consultants | Virtual Law Library™ | Action LawLine™ |
| Support Services | LawMall | Speak Up!™ |
| Bar Associations | LawLinks Forums | |
| Employment | | |

---

**Special Features**

 **Winning Moves Inc.** - Winning Moves' Judge 'n' Jury Trial. You are a member of the virtual jury for each week's new trial. Compare your verdict to the one rendered in the actual case.

 **Guest Authority of the Month**
**Henry Beck**

 **Law Mall: Highly rated Timeslips 6 For Windows(tm).**

**FIGURE 5–7B**

# DONNA BALLMAN
## FOR CIRCUIT COURT JUDGE

AV rated by Martindale-Hubbell Law Directory (Highest rating awarded)

### Education

University of Miami School of Law, J.D., Cum Laude, Law Review: Wellesley College, B.A., Political Science and Philosophy, Wellesley College Scholar honors (equivalent Magna Cum Laude).

### Employment

Donna M. Ballman, P.A., President of law firm. Commercial litigation, employment discrimination, election law. Florida Supreme Court certified circuit civil mediator, arbitrator.

### Honors

Names "Woman of the Year" by Downtown Business and Prof. Women; Listed in Who's Who in American Law, International Who's Who and Who's Who in the South and Southwest.

### Offices Held

Florida Bar, Judicial Evaluation Committee, 1993-present; Dade County Bar, ABA Host Committee, Chair, YLD Host Services Subcommittee, 1994-95; Grand Jury Association of Florida, Board, 1992-present; National Association of Women Business Owners Board, Co-chair Government Affairs Committee, 1991-92; Business and Professional Women, Downtown Miami Club, First Vice President, 1992-94; Florida Association for Women Lawyers, Board 1992-95; Chair, Legislative Committee, 1991-92

### Member

American Judicature Society, American Association of University Women, National Association of Women Business Owners, ABA Judicial Administration Division, Association of Trial Lawyers of America, American Arbitration Association, Downtown Business and Professional Women, Life Member National Council of Jewish Women, Omicron Delta Kappa honor society, Vizcayans, Smithsonian

**FIGURE 5–8A**

*After a very slow download, "On the Frontal Lobe of Technology" suggests pre-frontal lobotomy. The first line of text, "No, we haven't lost our minds" seems to recover, but then the text lapses back into weak generalities.*

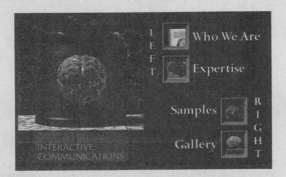

# On the Frontal Lobe of Technology

No, we haven't lost our minds. Nature has a very reliable way of organizing our thoughts. We count on our left hemisphere for thoughts of reason, intellect and analysis, while our right hemisphere is open to creativity, conceptualization and artistic vision.

DDB Needham Interactive Communications, is the new media and new technologies subsidiary of **DDB Needham Worldwide**.

As a marketing communications team, we're dedicated to the development and implementation of new media and new technologies to enhance **our clients'** ability to deliver an effective marketing message.

To make that happen, we've got **a great team** of multi-disciplined professionals who understand effective marketing, as well as technology, and know how to make both work to our client's advantage.

So, like the corpus callosum, DDB Interactive Communications is the link that joins the hemispheres of creativity with technical reason. So open up your mind and explore our vision.

Inside you'll find information about our agency network, our philosophy and vision, **samples** of our work and our **Gallery**, where you can see the "off-the-time-clock" endeavors of the creative geniuses who fill our halls. (Now Open: an exhibit by artist Suzanne Richard) *And, if you would like to be one of those who are filling our halls we invite you to take a look at our* **On-Line Opportunities**.

**FIGURE 5–8B**

We're very proud to be home to the Ad Council on the Internet. Click here for the Ad Council's Public Service Events Calendar, information about the Ad Council and how to receive free information about Public Service Campaigns.

Home | Who We Are | Expertise | Samples | The Gallery | E-Mail

Copyright © 1995 DDB NEEDHAM INTERACTIVE COMMUNICATIONS

**FIGURE 5–9**

*Another slow download—this time what appears to be the reception room of an advertising agency. If you were interviewing agencies, would you want to tour the office or would you look for timeliness, inventiveness, and stimulation?*

# Welcome to Winkler McManus

Let's get acquainted.
As you tour <u>our offices</u> we encourage you to leave no button unclicked.
No door unopened. No marketing pearl of wisdom unturned.
Enjoy.

## Getting Around

Click on the objects in our virtual lobby above or use the navigation bar below to explore our agency. We invite you to check out our <u>Staff Offices</u>, our <u>Portfolio</u>, our <u>Philosophy</u>, and <u>Late Breaking News</u>. Our special guests are also invited to join us in the <u>Boardroom</u> for a private presentation. We've even got a few hidden tidbits for your surfing pleasure. Click on the neon Winkler McManus Advertising sign above to find out more <u>about</u> this home page.

## Please visit our <u>Bibliothèque</u>

You will find links to some interesting resources on the Web that are related to Advertising and marketing. Enjoy.

Please take a minute to tell us about your feelings toward this <u>Sony logo</u>.
Thanks!

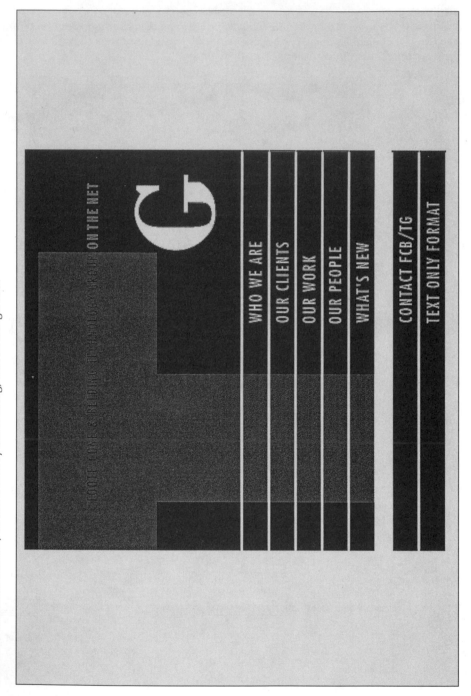

**FIGURE 5–10A**
*What about this home page suggests an understanding of Web-surfer demographics? Obviously the page is aimed not at casual drop-ins but at potential clients. On a competitive level, a "three-piece suit" approach holds dignity but may lose attention. That conclusion, in the world of advertising, can be dangerous.*

**FIGURE 5–10B**

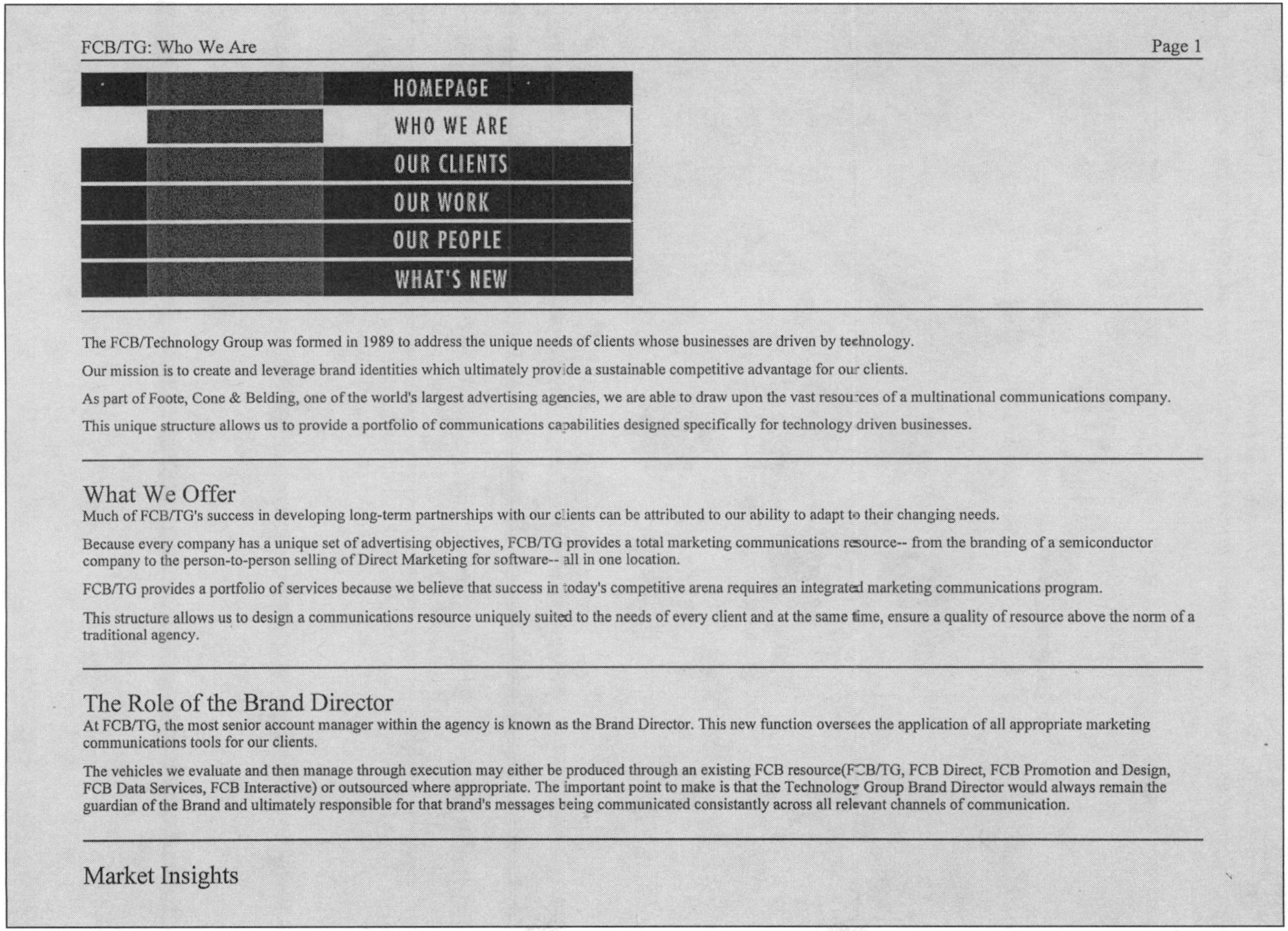

FCB/TG: Who We Are

Page 1

HOMEPAGE
WHO WE ARE
OUR CLIENTS
OUR WORK
OUR PEOPLE
WHAT'S NEW

The FCB/Technology Group was formed in 1989 to address the unique needs of clients whose businesses are driven by technology.

Our mission is to create and leverage brand identities which ultimately provide a sustainable competitive advantage for our clients.

As part of Foote, Cone & Belding, one of the world's largest advertising agencies, we are able to draw upon the vast resources of a multinational communications company. This unique structure allows us to provide a portfolio of communications capabilities designed specifically for technology driven businesses.

## What We Offer

Much of FCB/TG's success in developing long-term partnerships with our clients can be attributed to our ability to adapt to their changing needs.

Because every company has a unique set of advertising objectives, FCB/TG provides a total marketing communications resource– from the branding of a semiconductor company to the person-to-person selling of Direct Marketing for software– all in one location.

FCB/TG provides a portfolio of services because we believe that success in today's competitive arena requires an integrated marketing communications program.

This structure allows us to design a communications resource uniquely suited to the needs of every client and at the same time, ensure a quality of resource above the norm of a traditional agency.

## The Role of the Brand Director

At FCB/TG, the most senior account manager within the agency is known as the Brand Director. This new function oversees the application of all appropriate marketing communications tools for our clients.

The vehicles we evaluate and then manage through execution may either be produced through an existing FCB resource(FCB/TG, FCB Direct, FCB Promotion and Design, FCB Data Services, FCB Interactive) or outsourced where appropriate. The important point to make is that the Technology Group Brand Director would always remain the guardian of the Brand and ultimately responsible for that brand's messages being communicated consistantly across all relevant channels of communication.

Market Insights

**FIGURE 5–11**

*This advertising agency exhibits a knowledge of both the medium and its inhabitants. The page downloads fast because illustrations are small. It has no ponderosity. Mildly out of key with the cartoons is the no-nonsense list of links.*

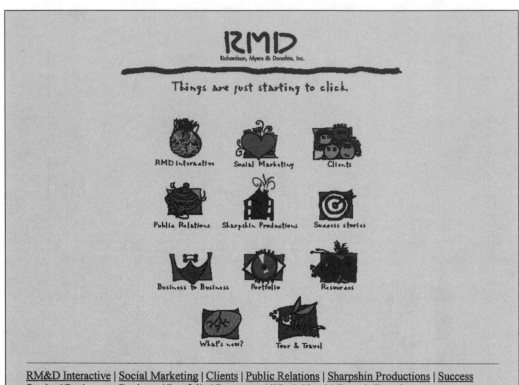

RM&D Interactive | Social Marketing | Clients | Public Relations | Sharpshin Productions | Success Stories | Business to Business | Portfolio | Resources | What's New? | Tour & Travel

*Richardson, Myers & Donofrio, Inc., 120 W. Fayette St., Baltimore, MD 21201/E-mail: rmd@rmd.com /Phone: (410) 576-9000/Fax: (410)528-8809 / Last revised: January 8, 1995 / Copyright© 1995 / Webmaster*

# 6 What (Almost) Always Works

One marketing principle always works. It's a universal truth:

**Adapt your marketing efforts to your potential customers' mindset. Think about what they want to buy, not about what you want to sell.**

This is the classic differential separating seller from buyer. The seller cares about what it is. The buyer cares about what it will do *for me*.

So if you want to develop Internet sales tactics that grab and shake the visitor to your Web site, start by figuring out what kinds of visitors you want to attract and think about what they're looking for. Deliver it . . . and you're in business.

Let's hyperlink back to Chapter Two, where we described these five different kinds of Web visitor:

- Directed Information Seekers
- Undirected Information Seekers

- Bargain Hunters

- Entertainment Seekers

- Directed Buyers

What will attract each of these? What will appeal to each of these?

The answer is only mildly complex. It's complex because no group is totally homogenized. It's mild because whether you're advertising on the Net, on a bulletin board, or in the daily newspaper, this same situation exists. Let's analyze logical appeals to each of these five target-groups.

# Directed Information Seekers

Directed Information Seekers want information. Well, so does everybody. But this group is after *specific* information, *timely* information, and absolutely *relevant* information.

From a marketing point of view, this seems simple enough. These individuals want specific, timely, relevant information about products and services you offer, or they wouldn't be squatting at your site. So provide it. Give them several different levels of detail. For each product and service provide an overview page, full descriptions, and detailed specifications. Design overview pages for on-line reading and your other pages to be printed or read off-line.

Don't make the mistake so many market-unconscious sites make—telling the visitor what you want to say, not what he or she wants to see. That key word *relevant* can overcome multiple deficiencies in art, in production, in vocabulary, in overall polish. But no amount of professional artistry, brilliant production, colorful vocabulary, or gleaming polish can overcome a lack of relevance.

Research shows typical car buyers fit this profile, spending more than a month researching their purchase. Chrysler (Figure 7–2) caters to this kind of buying care by providing lots of information about each automobile model it sells.

# MAKE YOURSELF EASY TO FIND

Register your site with every *relevant* directory you can find—not just Yahoo!, but whatever industry-specific directories your customers are likely to visit. To reach Directed Information Seekers, making yourself easy to find isn't complicated because you know in advance where these people are.

Most directories now use automated search-and-index programs. Make a list of every key word a customer may think of to find you. Then make sure you use every one of them someplace in your text. It's a simple rhetorical trick. If you're marketing cows, include words such as *cattle, bulls, bovine, milk, beef, herd, dairy—* any words that might relate directly or peripherally to what you're selling. You have no way of knowing what search-word your potential visitor will enter.

Be persuasive. Apply the rules of writing effective copy. These don't change because you're using a different medium. (See Chapter Seven for copywriting guidance.)

If you distribute a printed catalog, in its pages refer customers to your Web site for more information. Don't just bury this reference at the bottom of the page (although your URL should appear right next to your toll-free number). Also mention it in at least some of your catalog entries: "Want to know more about this product? Visit us on the World Wide Web at http://www.abc.com/productinfo/thisproduct."

Don't stop there! You've invited them in for a visit. Be home, with the curtains open, coffee hot, the welcome mat out, and a well-lit entranceway. Here is another circumstance in which you have to abandon your seller-attitude and adopt your buyer-attitude. *Why* does someone take you up on your offer to visit? If the offer to visit is sincere, back it up with an offer to do business—one that justifies the time spent seeking out your site.

Now, what if they want information you have, but which doesn't directly relate to products and services you offer? No question: Find a way to provide this information, too.

Why?

Several reasons. First, you've already established that these are your customers or potential customers. You can't sell to them if you can't communicate with them. Get them to regard your site as a place they should visit regularly by providing information they value. Statesmanship eventually pays off because it impresses the right people.

Whatever you do, don't compromise the integrity of the information they're getting from you by artificially morphing it into a sales pitch. You'll drive your customers away, never to return, the moment they spot your transparent ploy. Instead, make this information straightforward and informative. Then place "teaser" information about your related products and services *as separate elements* on the same pages.

As a final step, use other media to cross-promote your site.

Take another look at Kodak's Web site in Chapter Two (Figure 2–2). Despite the considerable dullness (at least, when Kodak's home page was visited prior to publication of this book), Kodak could gain significant marketing advantage by offering information on how to take better photographs. So long as their customers actually want the information Kodak has to offer, they'll come to visit. Each visit gives Kodak the opportunity . . . missed in the site illustrated . . . to market its photographic products and photofinishing services.

Clear? You don't have to *avoid* salesmanship when transmitting generic product-use information. You only have to separate it. Steak and chocolate pudding make for an excellent meal . . . but not when mixed together.

# Undirected Information Seekers

Think about the psychology of the Undirected Information Seeker. No, don't sneer. This is you when you read the newspaper each morning. What are we looking for?

We want *something* interesting. *Something* useful. *Something* we would not have found on our own. *Something* that can give us an edge . . . an advantage . . . an insight . . . *something unexpected*, a pleasant surprise.

Clarity has to enter the approach to Internet marketing. On the Web, with its polyglot patronage, The Clarity Commandment must reign supreme:

> When you choose words and phrases for sales communication, clarity is paramount. Don't let any other component of the communications mix interfere with it.

Delta Airlines, for example, has an offering called *Travelogue* on its Web site (Figure 6-1). The visitor wonders: What is *Travelogue?* It surely must be a mystery to most visitors, based on the actual home page. What edge, what advantage, does it represent? Using this as a criterion, visitors looking for vacation ideas might well get in the habit of visiting the Delta site on a regular basis. Since Delta's flight schedules are right there in another part of the site, the tie-in is a natural.

Approach this customer category with caution. Far too easily you can fall into the trap of turning your commercial Web site into a publishing hobby. Here's how you can turn the Undirected Information Seeker's psychology to your advantage:

> Define a few information categories that fit your business profile. These should be categories that change at least once a week; or even better, once a day or more. They should be categories potential customers *for your products and services* will find useful, interesting, novel, or amusing.

## BECOMING "THE PRIME SOURCE"

Where can you find a low-cost, low-effort way of obtaining the information? Many potential customers don't read all (or, for that matter, any) of the trade publications. They aren't privy to the day-to-day banter that helps your plant or office or store stay abreast of the marketplace. Even if they read beyond their own local daily newspaper, they may not have seen specific articles. And if they have, they may not have recognized the significance.

So a "Daily Digest" isn't difficult.

Correction: A Daily Digest isn't difficult at first. After a few months it can be an albatross around your corporate neck. If you start it, vow to stay with it for at least half a year.

While you're at it, make sure you clear any intellectual property hurdles. You won't do anyone any good if you publish information somebody else owns, protects, and screams about. But usually you're safe, because no one can copyright *fact*.

If you treat your Web site seriously, your potential customers will get into the habit of visiting you. So be sure to include, along with the items of interest you publish for their benefit, a brief sales pitch for one of your products, knowledge of how to order from you, how fast you ship, and the extra discount, service, or whatever you offer for Web customers only.

What you want is for these potential customers to have you in front position, both on their "hot list" and in their minds, so when they decide to buy, you and not your competitor are the one they naturally go to. After all, you're carefully instilling in them the knowledge that they'll get an extra discount, faster shipping, top-notch merchandise, or whatever you use to describe the advantages your products have over your competitors. As you implement this program, paste this sentence on your keyboard:

## Specifics outsell generalizations.

And, be sure they know how to reach you to place an order quickly and easily.

# Bargain Hunters (1)—The Search for Free *Stuff*

Bargain Hunters hear about this great *stuff* on the Internet, and they're out to find it. Why? Because they *want* it, of course; and it's free, or nearly so. Besides, if they accumulate enough of it, then all that free stuff ends up paying for their personal computer.

Will they actually use any of it? Maybe. They may find a share-ware enhancement to the Windows File Manager, and somehow forget to send in their registration and check for $35. They may meander over to NASA's Web site to download some snazzy pictures of Jupiter to use as Windows wallpaper.

Stock quotations are nice—and a bit more convenient and timely than looking for a hand-me-down copy of today's newspaper. The Microsoft Network (Figure 2–3) lets you customize its home page, giving you free information like this and a reason to come back frequently.

## PLAYING WITH . . . AND CONTROLLING . . . FIRE

When you cater to Bargain Hunters, you're playing with fire. Here's a test:

> **Juxtapose the profile we've just described with your target customer profile. If you believe you have significant overlap, hoist the red flags.**

Remember, you're not trying to maximize the number of visits to your site. That's Amateur Night. You're trying to maximize your site's contribution to your selling effort.

The good news about Bargain Hunters? They're easy to please. Just offer bargains. The bad news about Bargain Hunters? You have to figure out ways to convert them to buyers. The worse news? They may be the most populous subspecies on the Web, and courting them at the expense of more serious, more dedicated prospects can result in an unprofitable enclave on only Bargain Hunters. You won't make any money that way!

Fortunately, you're not dealing with a new situation. Sears faced it years ago. People all over the United States read the Sears catalog for its entertainment value. Sears didn't mind a bit because the entertainment consisted of dreaming you could own that stuff.

You can employ similar tactics. The details depend on what you have to offer. You can use one or more of the following.

*The Not-Quite-Good-Enough Gambit:* Offer low-resolution photographs free, and their high-resolution equivalents for a fee. Use this approach when you're selling downloadable intellectual property. Another version: give away the abstract but sell the whole article.

*The Good-Enough-For-Some-But-Not-For-You Maneuver:* Offer scaled-back, warty versions of software for free, and sell the "Professional Version," really a variation of the free version, for a reasonable profit.

*The Government Contracting Tactic:* Give them something that offers limited value by itself, and much greater value when used in conjunction with something else you also sell. "You know, that plane would fly much better with *engines*. We can add them for a modest additional cost." This approach has a lot of versatility. You can use it whenever you can link two products, one of which is a low-cost, low-margin item.

US News Online does something of the sort (Figure 6–2) by offering a free newsletter delivered by electronic mail. Presumably the newsletter serves to promote both the Web site itself and the printed magazine with the three products—newsletter, Web, and magazine—constructed to be complementary. As you can see, the "free" aspect is curiously restrained.

*The Gillette-Razor Coup:* Give away the instrument, sell the supply. Gillette gave the world a wonderful business model. Use it whenever you can. A popular variant in the software industry: give away the software; charge for the upgrade. Another popular variant: give away the software; charge for new clip-art. If it had to, Mattel could probably make money giving away Barbie dolls and selling only the outfits.

*The Game and Contest Attractor:* You don't have to give something to everyone. Games and contests have a long history in marketing.

Their interactivity means they'll adapt well to the Web. The Web's natural affinity for marketing databases closes the loop—assuming Bargain Hunters may also be buyers in other contexts.

Of everything you can do, games and contests will probably work best, so long as you can keep them fresh and sufficiently interesting without adding too much complexity. Trivia contests, simple crossword puzzles, a geography quiz, all can qualify. Probably they'll work better than a simple drawing, since they provide more interactivity and a sense that skill, wit, determination, or knowledge will count for something. An easy example: "Be the one who e-mails us the most words of four letters or more from our name, Abacus Computers, before January 31 and we'll send you a CD-ROM. . . ."

Delta (Figure 6–1) came close with its "Skyscrapers" game, a logical idea . . . although in the opinion of the authors of this book it missed a few key elements, which can damage its effectiveness. First, it doesn't explain *at once* that Skyscrapers is a game that offers anything to winners other than fun. Second, it demands that visitors fill out a one-page-long information form (and are any visitors so naive they don't understand this will put them on a mailing list?) before they can play the game. Third, it doesn't describe the prizes, leaving visitors to speculate on what they might win and whether it's worth the time and effort.

A powerful concept can lose pace when the originator views it through company eyes instead of visitor eyes.

*The TV-Commercial Method:* Offer anything at all for free, and force your visitor to sit through a sales presentation before giving them the goods. Use this when you do want to attract Bargain Hunters but don't have any strong, logical associations between something you can give away and your real products and services.

Using *Free* offers to attract visitors, like the Force in *Star Wars*, has a dark side. You have to keep on giving stuff away to generate repeat visits, and your visitors have little incentive to become buyers . . . unless you give them that incentive.

# Bargain Hunters (2)—The Search for *Bargains*

Some Bargain Hunters want . . . well, bargains. Discounts. Better deals through the Internet than they can get anywhere else.

Why not give them what they want?

At this writing few sites successfully sell directly on the Web, and there's a strong perception that the Web has few shoppers on it. That can easily lead to a herd mentality: Your competitors aren't doing it, so it must be wrong.

If the Web is chock-full of people looking for free stuff, why would you believe it has few discount shoppers?

Opinion: One reason few Internet visitors look for bargains is that bargains are hard to come by on-line. More often than not you can get better prices in a store. If you go to a discount mall looking for bargains and discover higher prices than you'd pay at Nieman Marcus, you won't go back.

The parallel is obvious: If word gets around that you offer real discounts and real convenience at your Web site, you'll get customers, even if they do decide to place their order through a toll-free number. How can you avoid it?

And why shouldn't you offer an extra discount? By using Web technology you can virtually (no pun intended) eliminate all transaction costs and data-entry errors. You can let your customers enter orders directly into your order-processing system. You'll save at least a few dollars per order. Pass some of them along.

Shrewd marketers know how to offer *apparent* bargains. This is a matter of perception rather than reality. Everyone knows (or actually may be) an individual who doesn't care what something costs; it's what that item has been reduced from.

You can offer other attractions for the difficult but omnipresent Bargain Hunter phylum. How about some of those mentioned for other groups? Games and contests are logical offers for this gang. Giveaways that accompany orders are another, and in fact everything that works for people looking for freebies will work here too. Bargain Hunters, in common with Directed Information Seekers, will also respond to more product information. Make it a mouse-click away from the product listing.

Bargain Hunters want to justify their investment in hardware, on-line charges and time, both to themselves, and sometimes to a spouse. Help them.

# Entertainment Seekers

Entertainment Seekers are in a sense mild Bargain Hunter mutants. They look for free stuff while paralleling the stereotypical Web surfer. They see the Web as an entertainment medium of vast breadth and potential, and they want to explore the medium before the masses get there.

It is remarkable that in the last decade of the twentieth century a medium that for the most part presents flat, static images, albeit in color, could become so popular, given the contrast with television. Almost beyond doubt the Web's popularity stems from the perception that it's free (despite monthly access costs on a par with cable TV and per-thousand costs for advertisers which can run well above other media) and the occasional reality of its interactivity.

The sad fact: entertainment is hard to come by on the Web, and the medium doesn't yet offer the technological underpinnings that will let it compete with television and movies on their own level.

## AMUSEMENT, NOT BEMUSEMENT

Still, a lot of potential customers are wandering around looking for a site that will amuse them. How can you give them exactly that?

One answer lies in that marvelous word *edutainment*. Yes, we're talking about Entertainment Seekers, not information seekers. That's okay. By providing education you'll make your visitors feel good about themselves. By making it entertaining, you'll keep their attention. The educational value mitigates the lack of broad-cast-quality production value.

Another answer lies in "cool stuff." Animations, sound clips, contests and games, screen-saver downloads. Access to databases. Control over database records.

Then there's old-fashioned good writing. Create a story line and serialize it.

The second most difficult part will be to hold an entertainment seeker's interest. The hardest will be to convert an entertainment seeker into a customer. Your best bet will be "advertainment"—advertising that sells your product while providing entertainment value. That's the common (and thoroughly tested and proved) "Infomercial" strategy in television advertising. It may work on the Internet, too. Just beware of the double-edged nature of using entertainment to attract visitors. As in television advertising, where cleverness can interfere with your selling message, so too can cleverness detract from selling on the Web.

# Directed Buyers

As was mentioned in Chapter Two, this group wants to buy something—now. If it's what you are selling, this should be easy. This is your customer. (You know who your customers are—What they want, What they like, What they need, Right?) Three words should work here: Ready. Aim. Fire! Or:

- Make sure that the benefits of buying from you (rather than a competitor) are clear.

- Make it easy to order and ship (See Chapter 10).

- Make the entire process—from selection to purchase—as easy as possible.

# What (Almost) Always Works

Follow these four steps and you should fare well in cyberspace:

1.  Define a profile of your intended audience—your current customer profile and your potential additional customers.

2.  Figure out what they're looking for on the Web.

3.  Deliver what they're looking for in a context that also lets you deliver a selling message.

4.  Make yourself easy to buy from.

Easy? Certainly not. If it were, every Internet marketer would be successful. Logical? Certainly so. Treat the Net as the individual medium it is, catering to individual idiosyncrasies in both the medium and its inhabitants.

**FIGURE 6–1A**

*The "Instant Win Entry Form" is a classic database enhancer, using incentives as the reason for gathering information.*

DELTA NEWS    FLIGHT PLAN    GATEWAYS    TRAVELOGUE    PLANE FUN

Worldwide Partners    SkyMiles        SkyScrapers

FAQ'S    Crown Rooms        BagTag

Phone-Numbers    Flight Schedules

Airports

Airplanes

This site has been optimized for Netscape and is in English only.

While you are traveling Delta Air Lines SkyLinks, you may leave the SkyLinks site and enter various independent web sites. During your visit, Delta Air Lines,Inc. is not responsible for either the content or nature of this linked site. Delta Air Lines conducts periodic reviews of all reciprocal links for vigilance of acceptable content and nature of the linked sites.

® 1995 Delta Air Lines, Atlanta, GA.

Comments and Suggestions: webmaster@delta-air.com

**FIGURE 6–1B**

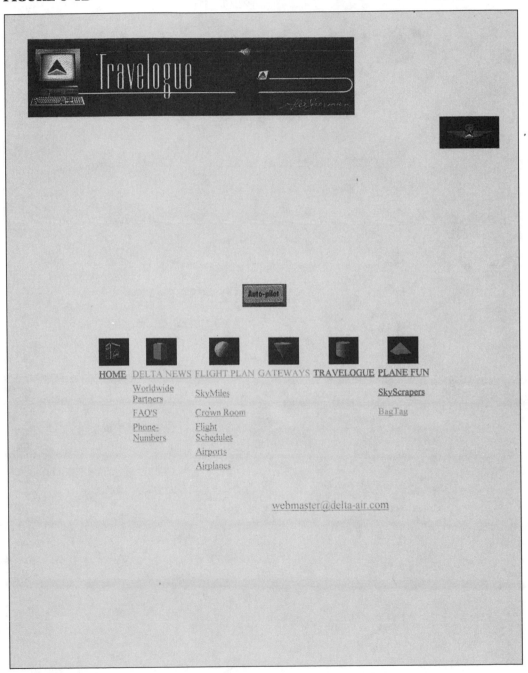

**FIGURE 6–1C**

## INSTANT WIN ENTRY FORM

Before you play SKYSCRAPERS, please provide Delta with following information:

1. Are you a member of Delta SkyMiles?  Yes  No

2. If yes, please fill in your SkyMiles #  and skip to question 4.

3. If no, would you like to register to be a SkyMiles Member?  Yes  No

4. Are you a member of another Frequent Flyer program?  Yes  No

                    If yes, which ones: please check the appropriate boxes

        **American Airlines** AAdvantage
        **USAir** Frequent Traveler
        **Continental** OnePass
        **Northwest** WorldPerks
        **TWA** Frequent Flight Bonus
        **United** Mileage Plus
        **SAS** Frequent Flyer EuroBonus Program
        **Canadian** Canadian Plus
        **Air Canada** Aeroplan
        **Alaska Airlines** Mileage Plan
        **British Airways** Executive Club
        **Other**

5. Please check the box that most accurately reflects your flying habits.
    I fly more than 20 business trips per year
    I fly between 5 and 20 business trips per year
    I fly less than 5 business trips per year

Title
First Name
Last Name
Home
Address 1
Home
Address 2
City          State Zip:

**FIGURE 6–1D**

Home Phone     Home E-mail

Prizes will only be sent to the above registered address.

Thank you for taking the time to fill out the information.

## Good Luck!

HOME   DELTA NEWS   FLIGHT PLAN   GATEWAYS   TRAVELOGUE   PLANE FUN

|  |  |  |
|---|---|---|
| Worldwide Partners | SkyMiles | SkyScrapers |
| FAQ'S | Crown Room | BagTag |
| Phone-Numbers | Flight Schedules | |
| | Airports | |
| | Airplanes | |

Comments and Suggestions: webmaster@delta-air.com

**FIGURE 6–2A**

*This site combines late news, commentary, and advertising. Because the advertising is easily bypassed, visitors won't resent commercializing a site dedicated to information. Note the "Free Newsletter." In addition to the e-mail address, the subscriber provides a street address and phone—pure database.*

# Welcome to U.S.News Online.

Click here to enter the enhanced version of U.S.News Online. Those on non-Netscape browsers or slow connections might find it better to navigate starting with the text-based version of our site.

Visiting our site via CompuServe, America Online, or the Microsoft Network? You can still use Netscape. Click here for details.

This site is enhanced with:

U.S.News Online is ranked in the
Top 5% of the Web by Point Communications!
See what others are saying about U.S.News Online.

**FIGURE 6–2B**

MAIN EVENTS

- ▸ **NEWS WATCH**
- ▸ **WASHINGTON CONNECTION**
- ▸ **NEWS YOU CAN USE**®
- ▸ **COLLEGES & CAREERS**
- ▸ **TOWN HALL**
- ▸ **THIS WEEK'S ISSUE**

OUTLOOK
COLUMNISTS
U.S. NEWS
WORLD REPORT
BUSINESS & TECH
CULTURE & IDEAS
NEWS YOU CAN USE

HIGHLIGHTS

▸ **ELECTION '96**

## Battle for the GOP

Buchanan's win heralds new coalition

▸ **COVER STORY**

## Failing Our Children

How teachers' unions are holding back schools

**EXTRA, EXTRA:**

NEWSWATCH: Telecom turmoil: A cyber protest over the new law.
NEWS YOU CAN USE: New! Get instant updates on stocks and mutual funds.
TOWN HALL: An interview with Netscape's Jim Clark

GET OUR FREE NEWSLETTER

MAIN MENU |  SEARCH | NEWS WATCH | WASHINGTON CONNECTION | NEWS YOU CAN USE | COLLEGE FAIR | TOWN HALL | ISSUE

**FIGURE 6–2C**

# Newsletter

**Get your FREE newsletter from U.S.News Online**

Want to know the latest hot news, politics and consumer information on our site? Subscribe to our free newsletter and get on the fast track to U.S.News Online. Each week we'll send you the latest highlights from our service, sneak previews of hot columns such as Washington Whispers and John Leo, and other special offerings. Best of all, you can get our newsletter in HTML format, so all you have to do is click and go!

```
Name:

Email Address:

Street Address:

City:      State:  Zip:

Daytime Phone:
```

MAIN MENU | SEARCH | NEWS WATCH | WASHINGTON CONNECTION | NEWS YOU CAN USE | COLLEGE FAIR | TOWN HALL | ISSUE

CREDITS

Send comments to webmaster@usnews.com

© Copyright U.S. News & World Report, Inc. All rights reserved.

This site is engineered by AGTinteractive

**FIGURE 6–3**

*This site asks visitors to sign its Guest Book, clearly a database-building ploy. Why? Veteran surfers know the usual result: a stream of e-mailed solicitations. A marketing maxim that's reasonably foolproof in any medium: Offer something to get something.*

 # Long vs. Short Copy, and Related Factors

A parable:

> Some day the Net will settle down. All the major providers will
> agree on standards, and the smaller providers will go along
> because they have to.

> Text will run in standard lengths. Illustrations will be in stan-
> dard positions. Product and corporate identification will be in
> standard places. Visitors will have eye-comfort, knowing what to
> expect.
> Then some maverick will break the rules.
> Suddenly a visitor to that maverick's site *won't* know what to
> expect. And you know what? That site will become popular—and
> probably win some awards—just because it's different. (After all,
> conventional advertising bestows awards for "being different,"
> whether the difference results in business or not.)
> That's where the parable ends and reality begins.

In this case, one key word destroys any slavish desire for sameness: *Competition*. Competition isn't just for business because business is a result that never occurs when a business prospect:

1.  Doesn't see your sign;

2.  Can't enter your store because he or she doesn't see your sign;

3.  Even if he/she sees your sign, he/she ignores your store if your sign is the same size, color, and intensity as every other sign.

So that upstart will have an automatic edge, regardless of what the message may be, because the home page will have defeated the spectre of sameness.

Now: Hold it! Remember one of Murphy's Laws? "Professionals are predictable . . . it's the amateurs who are dangerous."

Beware the Rule of Mis-aimed Advertising:

### The cult, "That which is different = that which is good," is an infection as often as it is a cure.

The Internet has become a quick and convenient haven for those who prefer "difference" to "salesmanship." It's a natural step in the accelerated evolutionary process because—as was the case when television burst onto the national scene in the 1950s and, before that, when radio became a major factor in the 1920s—the medium literally *is* the message in a medium's formative stages.

The early surfers taught the early Internet marketers a profound lesson: They embraced enthusiastically any site that was "different" . . . and they didn't buy.

# Positive Rules for Copy Length

So as Internet marketing moves into its second generation, we have a more positive set of rules. For this chapter, we can project Four Rules of Copy Length.

The First Rule of Copy Length:

**Total copy length is not a negative factor. Substantial copy length within a single copy-block is a negative factor.**

The First Rule is a good friend to those who seriously regard the Net as a competitive means of getting the phone to ring. They have a story to tell, and the story has to pay off in business, not in unregistered "hits."

So they need copy—maybe lots of copy. But they're smart enough marketers to recognize the First Rule. Their copy is broken into chewable bites. The prospect gradually qualifies himself/herself as each copy block explains benefits and separates potential buyers from casual stoppers-in.

That's where The Second Rule of Copy Length is the great dividing line between an Internet presenter and an Internet marketer:

**Don't be afraid to sell.**

All very well; but the Second Rule, without the Third Rule, can be an irritant. The Third Rule:

**With every headline, every sentence, ask yourself: If I were reading this instead of writing it, would my interest level stay high?**

Some marketers have quite a valid point when they ignore the Third Rule, claiming the Second Rule is ample ammunition for the serious buyer. The Third Rule, after all, can lapse into entertainment. No, not *lapse* because, as this book has pointed out in previous chapters, the optimum is *edutainment*, and entertainment is half the word. But entertainment without sell is best left to the on-line services. If you're paying for a Web site, the Web site has to pay you back. Any other way of keeping score is an excuse.

## FORCING THE SECOND AND THIRD RULES TO MARRY ON YOUR HOME PAGE

Two sets of marriage vows exist, binding the Second and Third Rules. The first is to have a home page loaded with short, provocative subheads, not all of which are bald attempts to sell.

For example, you might have a "Joke of the Day," as many sites have. You might have a Peephole Special. You might salute the Customer of the Day (with a mild freebie if that customer calls before the day is out). You can offer something free or have a sweepstakes. You certainly can (and probably should) have a combination of *unlike* features, such as these, in concert. But none suggests long copy on the home page.

Figure 7–1A and B are low-resolution printouts of two SkiNet pages. The first, the home page, has a "grabber" in the center— "WIN A FREE TRIP!" A second home page, not shown here, is identical with one big difference. It says, "Click here—HOT QUIZ." Which is most likely to get that click?

The perennial strength of the word "Free" makes this the winning choice. A quiz is mildly logical when aimed at an in-group; but this is the Internet, and a quiz is second banana to a free trip.

Notice the copy just above the changeable insert:

Please send us feedback and join the SkiNet mailing list.

Now imagine how much more potent this message would be— and it's a crucial message because it's the name-claimer—if the copy had indicated a nominal benefit for feedback and offered a reason to join the mailing list. What would have been added to the mixture is another magical word: *Motivation*.

And motivation is the key to the Fourth Rule of Copy Length:

**Copy length can expand in ratio to the amount of promise it makes.**

Under the aegis of the Fourth Rule, that Spartan sentence might have been expanded to something such as this:

Hey! Send us feedback. You might wind up in print! And if you'll get on our mailing list (just enter your name and address two pages down), you'll get notifications of private sales, other special offers, and discount ski-trips.

More than twice as long. More than twice as potent.

Moving to the next page (Figure 7–1B), we see an offer to subscribe. The small illustrations—the covers of *Ski* and *Skiing for Women* magazines—take almost no time to download. Seven bullets give the surfer quick choices. A click on any of these and the surfer becomes a visitor—with the possibility of a subscription greatly improved.

The naked "SUBSCRIBE NOW!", with neither a subscription rate nor any apparent means of subscribing, wouldn't survive a basic Internet copywriting class. We might add a rule peripherally related to copy length:

**When you ask for action, be sure you've given your visitor
a means of action.**

Is *anything* about this SkiNet subscription page clever? Far from it. In fact, apparently this page is deliberately anti-clever. But a critical analysis shouldn't assume automatically—and mistakenly—that non-cleverness or deliberate anti-cleverness is a negative factor. Overly "clever" copy that calls attention to itself *as copy* can damage response.

## THE TENUOUS RELATIONSHIP BETWEEN CLEVERNESS AND RESPONSE

Will lack of bright copy hurt response? This is a complex question because the target group is *vertical* rather than *horizontal*. That is, all who land at that site have an implicit, advance interest in the subject. The need for clever courtship does not exist, since interest in the subject is predetermined. A venerable and safe philosophy is that brightness is always an asset. Cleverness can be a detriment when approaching a vertical-interest group who take the subject seriously.

That is only a partial answer, in today's Short Attention-Span Theatre. The Web surfer has many parallels with the recipient of targeted mail and special-interest magazines. But at least as many differences exist, most of them relating to the ambience. This is, after all, the Internet. The dedicated skier has easier means of connecting with the magazines than plowing through on-screen menus.

So the lack of cleverness probably won't hurt response, and it probably won't help response.

Don't think this means the page, as is, is optimal. Any analysis that concludes "It won't hurt and it won't help" automatically implies that a more stimulating approach *would* help.

What, for example?

Not the bullet copy, as we'll point out in a moment. Bullet copy has its own sets of rules, and cleverness is a difficult and often self-mutilating adjunct. In this example we have three candidates: the disembodied "SUBSCRIBE NOW!"; the open space into which the page might have added some excitement; and the line describing *Skiing for Women:*

> *Skiing for Women,* by the editors of *Skiing Magazine,* features fitness routines, reviews of skis and boots designed for women, health and beauty, a guide to women's ski weeks, and more.

A few adjectives in this copy block would help avoid any subordinating implication. When spinning off an ancillary, whether in publications or in product, the vendor should isolate without suggesting a junior position. So *"Skiing for Women,* by the editors of *Skiing Magazine,"* implies that *Skiing* is primary and *Skiing for Women* is secondary because the original magazine is presented as Big Brother. For the Internet—which treasures female surfers—this might have been better presented as, *"Skiing for Women* is a specialty *Skiing Magazine* publication."

Remember the very first Rule of Internet Advertising, from Chapter Two.

### Stop the surfer in his/her tracks.

This 31-word sentence describing *Skiing for Women* has chosen a sequence:

- fitness routines
- reviews of skis and boots designed for women
- health and beauty
- a guide to women's ski weeks
- "more"

Eliminating the neutral "more," which phrase has the greatest appeal—recognizing that the appeal is to a woman who has reached this site *not* accidentally?

The answer lies in yet another rule that applies to all media but is crucial for the Internet because of this medium's characteristics:

### Specifics outpull generalizations.

If you accept this rule as valid, you accept as valid the dominance of the two specific benefits ("reviews of skis and boots designed for women" and "a guide to women's ski weeks") over the two generalized benefits ("fitness routines" and "health and beauty"). The word *more* is at best semi-professional.

So this copy-block might have led with one of the two specifics. And leading with a specific suggests a *longer* description, because "reviews of skis and boots designed for women" has no brightness . . . and is, in fact, *less* specific than any reference to an individual ski or boots would have been. " 'Femmes Only' Weeks at Aspen and Vail" would have been both brighter and more specific than "a guide to women's ski weeks." Under the Internet copywriting formulae, it probably would have resulted in greater surfer-conversion to visitor.

# Rules for "Bullet" Copy

Bullet copy is terse . . . or it isn't bullet copy.

Figure 7–1A has seven bullets. Each of them, to the dedicated skier, is worth a click of the mouse. Being worth a click is the ultimate litmus test, transcending any other consideration.

Of the seven, one is less terse than the others. Take another look at Figure 7–1A and decide which one it is. While you're there, decide whether the extra verbiage helps or hurts.

If you chose the fifth bullet—"Gold Medal Resorts: The Top 10. How they got there, how they stay there," we agree with you. "How they  got there, how they stay there" drains impact. Visualize this bullet as it might have been truncated: "Gold Medal Resorts: The Top 10." Without the power-draining qualifiers, this bullet is more click-worthy.

Figure 7–1C is another page for this same magazine. Seven subheads (the seventh is adjacent to the cartoon at the bottom), each one no-nonsense and with minimal wording. Five of them lead to a single descriptive sentence. The other two need no further description. By removing the qualifying descriptions from the subheads themselves, both potency and synchronicity with the visitor's demand for quick choices are undimmed.

Figure 7–2 asks, "How do you want *your* home page today?" and then gives these bright and disarming bullets as choices: "Wow, this is better than squeezable cheese!" . . . "Hey, can I use this too?" One bullet needs a proofreader: " . . . what do I do know? (sic)" This page points up a logical suggestion: If you use bullets, make them prominent and easy to mouse-click. Scattering them may result in the visitor missing the very one he or she would have seized as a point of prime interest.

Separating descriptions from quickly grasped bullets first seizes the reader's attention and then justifies that seizure. For the Internet, it's a sound technique.

Bullets and the Internet are an instinctive match. Bullets are terse; surfers are impatient. Bullets are specific; surfers want specifics.

# Simplicity versus Sophistication

Many copywriters want to seem sophisticated. They polish phraseology until it gleams like fine poetry. They check the thesaurus before settling on any adjective.

When writing for the Internet, this can be a mistake.

Why? Because of the two reasons we have mentioned so often:

1. The "let's get to the point" attitude of most surfers.

2. The Internet's greater parallel with classified advertising than with display advertising.

Colorful prose invariably is longer than concise prose. As the Internet expands into many mini-niche-markets, far beyond its already fragmented universe, the writer will have an easier time making a conscious choice. Recognizing that categorizing is simplistic, Internet marketers can at worst implement generalized criteria, choosing copy-approaches based on factors such as these:

- Automobiles—sophisticated

- Business-to-business—simple

- Computers and electronics—simple

- Entertainment—simple

- Fashion—sophisticated

- Financial—simple, with terminology matching the best targets

- Food—simple for staples, sophisticated for exotics

- Fund raising—simple

- Houses—sophisticated

- Lifestyle—simple for the under-35s, sophisticated for the over-35s

- Liquor—sophisticated

- Office products—simple

- Sports—simple

- Subscriptions—simple for all but "posturing" publications

- Toys—simple for end-user, sophisticated for adult buyer

- Travel—sophisticated

Most of these are obvious, except to the determined copywriter more concerned with personal image than with marketing. Some are mildly abstruse. For example, fund raising is categorized "simple." This is because any fund raiser unable to describe the cause and generate empathy with simple language won't succeed on the Net.

# Let the Third Rule Guide You

The Third Rule can transform a journeyman writer into the king or queen of Internet copy:

**With every headline, every sentence, ask yourself: If I were reading this instead of writing it, would my interest-level stay high?**

One assumption has to be in place. The writer has to know who the best targets are. In order to do that, the writer has to have a working knowledge of what he or she is trying to sell.

With those bits of knowledge in place, no excuse for mis-aiming the copy, through length or refinement, is acceptable.

**Chewable bites, please.**

Figure 7–3 (A–E) is an example of long copy and long paragraphs. This was the Chrysler home page, then linked (randomly on our part) to the 1996 Town & Country minivan.

The home page is relatively standard. Once in Town & Country territory, the visitor is confronted by paragraphs of forbidding length. What obviously has happened is that a non-communicator picked up copy from brochures not intended for direct adaptation to the Net.

Breaking the text into chewable bites involves no major communication skills. The assumption that someone who wants information will endure visual hardship to get that information is sometimes correct. But in a competitive ambience, it sometimes is incorrect. Why gamble by testing visitors' interest spans?

This site shows why those whose familiarity with the Web is only peripheral shouldn't be surprised when a major marketer sets up a site with thousands of pages. Here, the visitor can bypass what he/she doesn't want to see and zero in on absolute specifics that otherwise would require a visit to a dealer showroom.

By providing all this information, the manufacturer adds a confidence-factor, so when the visitor comes into the showroom much of the time that might have been spent in *explanation* can be switched to a higher-octane *selling demonstration*.

The caveat that makes sense regardless of number of pages: Never does a site have an excuse for being hard to read.

**FIGURE 7–1A**

*Prominence of "Win a free trip" . . . late weather forecasts . . . and quick availability of information from the top two skiing magazines assure this site of steady attendance by those interested in this sport. The word* Free *is a can't-miss grabber; but a reason for "feedback" unquestionably would enhance response, as would specifics in place of the many generalizations.*

Check out <u>What's New</u> at SkiNet !

Welcome to SkiNet, an online service offering information on how to ski better, where to go, what to buy, as well as the latest news, weather, and race results. SkiNet draws upon the editorial expertise of the world's two best-selling ski publications, <u>Ski Magazine</u> and <u>Skiing Magazine</u>, to provide you with the most authoritative source of skiing information on the web.

Please <u>send us feedback</u> and <u>join the SkiNet mailing list</u>.

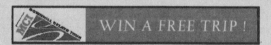

 ## <u>Skiing Magazine</u>

☐ **1996 Buyer's Guide to skis, boots, bindings**
☐ **Private Lessons: Skiing's world renowned instruction series**
☐ **The Skiing 100: America's best ski instructors**
☐ **Money-saving travel tips**

<u>**SUBSCRIBE NOW!**</u>

 ## <u>Ski Magazine</u>

☐ **Gold Medal Resorts: The Top 10. How they got there, how they stay there**
☐ **Sourcebook for great bargains and travel tips**
☐ **Up to the minute news on the US Ski Team**

<u>**SUBSCRIBE NOW!**</u>

**FIGURE 7–1B**

## Special Issue: <u>Skiing for Women</u>

**Skiing for Women, by the editors of Skiing Magazine, features fitness routines, reviews of skis and boots designed for women, health and beauty, a guide to women's ski weeks, and more.**

<u>Gear</u> | <u>News</u> | <u>Technique</u> | <u>Snowreport</u> | <u>Shop</u> | <u>Competition</u> | <u>Travel</u> | <u>Community</u>
<u>Ski Magazine</u> | <u>Skiing Magazine</u>

SkiNet is a production of Times Mirror Magazines. All rights reserved.

Hosting services provided by <u>the Internet Plaza</u>.

**FIGURE 7–1C**

*This clean-looking page has two advantages: it obviously takes no time to scan—and make a selection—and it has both clarity and specificity without verbosity. Visitors who want additional information check any of the seven subheads. The link then has considerable text, but the very nature of clicking the mouse on one of these changes the mind-set to anticipation of what follows.*

---

Welcome to Ski Magazine

**Travel**

**Results from our annual Reader Resort Survey**
SKI readers rate the top 80 resorts.

**The Skier's Guide to Europe**
Ready, Set, Euro: a guide to get you on your way.

**Going Places**
The Ski Holiday Sourcebook for great bargains and travel tips.

**Instruction**

**Be Strong To Ski Strong**
The Boomer Skier: keeping (or getting) youthful strength with plyometrics and anaerobic training.

**Gear**

**SKI Test 1995**
We tested over 300 skis. Full results here, plus winning skis (now on sale) from the 1994 SKI Test.

**FIGURE 7–2**

*Hot graphics and entertaining bullet copy make this a great home page. Any criticism? If you are going to use bullets, make them big and attention-getting.*

**FIGURE 7–3A**

*How much information does the visitor want . . . and about which model does he/she want it? Positives: This site is a classic example of why depth can be close to limitless, and the visitor has no trouble finding the sought-after information. Negatives: The Town & Country "Features" link (Figure 7–3D) is in need of paragraphing, and some descriptions are coldly clinical.*

# Welcome to The Chrysler Home Page

## ... and welcome to the family

In a span of barely three years, an entirely new line of Chrysler automobiles has been created. It began with a design/engineering concept called Cab Forward -- a totally new architecture for the automobile which has produced roomier sedans with greater stability and roadability.

Integrating Chrysler's traditional luxury features into stylish Cab-Forward design and quality-engineered value retention, this new family of refined automobiles is arguably the most owner-thoughtful lineup ever conceived.

Please take a serious ... but leisurely ... look at Cirrus, Concorde, Chrysler LHS, Town & Country, Sebring Coupe and the all-new Sebring Convertible.

The recent reintroduction of this seal reflects a renewal of the design leadership and innovative engineering that the badge symbolized for more than seven decades.

## The Chrysler Lineup

 **Cirrus**
It's not just a step above. It's a new plateau.

**FIGURE 7–3B**

 **LHS**
The performance, engineering and quality of a European road car.

 **Town & Country**
The ultimate in minivan luxury, safety and engineering.

 **Sebring Convertible**
Racy enough to entertain your dearest fantasies.
Roomy enough to entertain your nearest friends.

 **Sebring**
The cure for the common coupe.

## Other Areas of Interest

 Special Offers

 Customer One

 1-800 FOR-A-CHRYSLER

**FIGURE 7–3C**

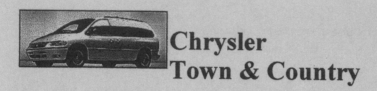

**Chrysler
Town & Country**

*Click the image for a larger view*

---

☐ **Town & Country LXi**

☐ **Town & Country LX**

☐ **Town & Country**

☐ **Features**

---

[ Cirrus ] [ Concorde ] [ LHS ] [ Town & Country ] [ Sebring ] [ Sebring Convertible ]
[ 1-800 ] [ Special Offers ] [ Customer One ] [ Other Chrysler Sites ]

---

*If you have comments on this web site, contact the webmaster at: chryslercars@chryslercars.com*
*© Copyright 1995-96 Chrysler Corporation.*
*All Rights Reserved.*

**FIGURE 7–3D**

# Chrysler Town & Country

## Features

Luxury amenities never before found in a minivan are standard. All the electronics of the leading luxury sedans are part and parcel of Town & Country LXi. It begins as you open the door. Unique Personalized Remote Entry System enables two drivers to pre-p rogram settings for their personal power seat and power mirror positions for instant recall. Both front seats are easily eight-way adjustable (including recliner feature), via power actuators shaped for an instinctive "feel" and touch-logic quickness. Naturally, all seating is designed to provide an optimal blend of comfort and ergonomic support for the long distances you'll find yourself wanting to drive Town & Country. AM stereo*/FM stereo cassette and CD player is standard on the LXi model, available on others. I t features easy-to-access control of all functions -- for listening enjoyment without having to memorize confusing computer-like operating sequences. Electrochromic inside rearview mirror automatically dims the reflection of bright headlights from following cars. Dual Zone Temperature Controls enable the driver and passenger to dial up their own climate "zone." (Rear seat passengers are served by area-specific heating and air conditioning outlets.) Thoughtfulness abounds within Town & Country LXi, from an intelligently reinvented steering column stalk and wheel which locates many control functions at your fingertips to a convenient lockable side-of-sea t compartment, just one of many such storage locations. And Town & Country is one of the quietest Chrysler minivans ever -- the result of advanced technology in controlling noise and vibration.
*Some AM stereo broadcasting may not be compatible with this radio.*

Luxury that is useful is an attribute unique to Town & Country. Today's active lifestyles practically shout for versatility in a luxury vehicle, so get ready to make use of your seven-passenger Town & Country in ways you wouldn't even dream of using a luxury sedan, or even a limousine. Luxury engineering means making things work without a hassle. Easy Out Roller Seats(TM) are an example, making the conversion from rear seating to cargo carrying less demanding of upper body strength. Eight rollers glide each rear seat as it is unlatched, and molded tracks in the floor guide the s eat and reduce resistance to rolling. Multiposition bench seat recliners, along with three-position fore-and-aft adjustment for the rear bench, provide accommodation to personal preference, even in seven-passenger configuration. In fact , there are many seating configurations (see examples below), and the rear seats can be folded for increased cargo capability when it is not convenient to remove them. Removable Quad Command individual seats are optional (standard on LXi) in the intermedi ate seating position. The quad seats have armrests, and recline 66 degrees in three-degree increments for highly personalized comfort, and fold flat for cargo stowage/table use. All in all, Town & Country front and rear seats provide more versatility than ever before. Leather Quad Command seats are standard on LXi, optional on Town & Country and LX.
*Easy Out Roller Seats is a trademark of Chyrysler Corporation.*

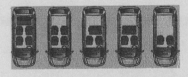

*Many seating/cargo configurations are possible by*

# 8 Tailoring Your Offers to the Net

The Internet is a paradoxical medium. It is at once the most sophisticated communications tool ever invented . . . and the most primitive in its psychological impact.

So the advertising or marketing practitioner who views the Net as "just another medium" and whose messages are pickups from newspapers or magazines or direct mail is at a disadvantage.

Being at a disadvantage by ignoring the medium *as a medium* doesn't mean the messages won't draw surfers . . . and won't convert surfers into visitors. In fact, the power of the message may bring business. The disadvantage lies in not maximizing impact . . . because maximizing impact is what professional salespeople do.

Visualize an advertiser whose television commercials are adaptations of his newspaper ads. The same weakness that stems from failure to exploit the uniqueness of television is the weakness infecting a lot of Internet advertising.

Two keys help you tailor your message to the Net. In combination, they represent the difference between this and any other medium of communication.

# The First Key: "Page One"

As is true of broadcast media, the Internet offers a benefit to the smaller marketer. General Motors and IBM may have thousands of pages, but the tiniest home page has *equality*. When the surfer lands on that page, it's Page One—the *only* page, the *only* image on the computer screen.

All sites are created equal. All sites have the same initial opportunity. The site that cost $2,000,000 to create has no edge over the site that cost $2,000 to create . . . until and unless that money translates into visitor-interest.

To the many millions of casual consumer prospects, and in a great deal of business-to-business marketing, company size is irrelevant. Budget allocated to site creation is worse than irrelevant—a huge budget seems to be an irresistible temptation to dump huge numbers of Web pages into an impossible-to-navigate site, as a substitute for salesmanship. In fact, both these factors—company size and Web budget—are far and away less important than downloading time. So the opportunity to stop the surfer in his/her tracks has no direct relationship with corporate size or budget.

Thus, the Net becomes a democratizer, an equalizer. Corporate size becomes subordinate to ingenuity.

This is especially true when planning to use the Net the way the individual with fist firmly on the mouse expects it to be used. That person expects stimulation. That person expects excitement. That person expects to see a reason for the page existing at all. That person expects a personalized contact.

Which leads us directly to . . .

# The Second Key: Interactive

Compounding the communicative mistake some advertisers make is ignoring the ambience. It's a get-together, not a lecture.

An example is Figure 8–1. Wine selection has often been a haven for snobbery, but this site de-mystifies it. And "Ask the Cork Dork" (the fourth item in the list) is both disarming and a non-threatening invitation to interactivity.

Publishers of periodicals learned decades ago that involvement improves the pull of subscription mailings. "Place your 'Free Issue' Sticker here" is a venerable technique. Many—no, most—subscription mailers hate the device. But they use it, because it works.

Why does it work? The psychological reasons are murky, but probably it's because the subscriber becomes a partner, not a passive quarry. The subscriber feels he or she has made the decision instead of having had it made for him or her. The subscription becomes a partnership, and the typical next-day "Buyer's Remorse" can't exist because by placing that sticker in its proper place the subscriber has been part of the sales generating process.

Asking questions—specific questions—is implicitly interactive. The marketer who can (ostensibly) create a question-driven home page is far more likely to convert a surfer into a visitor than is the marketer who presents text for reading or pictures for viewing. Now, why is that word *ostensibly* in parentheses? Because even though the concept of having a question-driven page is enticing, the mechanics and electronics involved may be beyond the marketer's budget. So although the page is *apparently* question-driven, actually the advance into the "meat" of the site is predetermined.

A point here: The inane "We want your feedback" is not a question, neither grammatically nor in terms of impact. You'll get more free-form response by presenting your e-mail address at the bottom of your home page. Why more? Immediacy—visitors don't have to wait for yet another page to finish downloading before offering their wisdom to you. In fact, "We want your feedback" can *suppress* response by appearing to demand that someone structure an opinion when none, in fact, exists. The site visitor may well depart rather than participate.

"Click here if you . . ." is a completely satisfactory substitute for questions. Note the word "you" in this mixture. It's the "you" component that turns the interactive key.

# Remember the Global Nature of the Medium

Internet marketers sometimes are stunned, in the early days of their participation, by getting inquiries from other countries. They shouldn't be, because the Net knows no national boundaries (a point not lost on nationalistic politicians, who use it to generate fear among their constituents).

The caution here isn't the one that applies to television spots broadcast to a trans-global audience, in which price conversion to pounds and marks and crowns and pesos and yen and baht are *de rigueur.* Pricing in U.S. dollars is standard on the Net for U.S. marketers.

When one sees a price in pounds—"£3.95"—one knows it's a company in the U.K. Unless that company also includes a dollar figure, the sale might be lost. But the U.S. dollar conversion rate is so widely known that the reverse problem doesn't seem to exist.

Then what is the caution?

It's argot. Jargon. Slang.

If you want an international response, use terminology a language translator can handle. One site had as its heading:

You'll go ballistic over this!

Another:

Let it all hang out.

Can't you see brows furrowing in bewilderment at these? Careful marketers know how to be conversational without lapsing into in-talk. Realize, please, that even some of the slang stemming from World War II more than half a century ago—*jerk, nut-case, bonkers*—is impenetrable to Internet users in other countries.

A controverting point: Don't aim your message at the smallest prospect segment. If what you're selling and the people to whom you're selling it are purely within your country's borders, *then* let it all hang out.

A simple solution for marketers whose image fits slang vocabulary: Create a multilingual, or even multinational home page that lets visitors choose their preferred language. From that point forward the rules are the same as for any other multinational promotion in which slang vocabulary appears: Employ native speakers from each country (not just each language) to check and repair your usage.

# The Advantage of "Today Only" Offers

Where else can you change your offer as fast as your fingers can hit the keyboard?

The only medium with as speedy a turnaround is radio . . . where, if necessary, an advertiser can ad lib a quick commercial within minutes after the motivation for the commercial occurs:

> Hi, this is Jack Russell of Russell Motors. As I'm talking, the trailer truck is unloading the most gorgeous silver BMW I've ever seen. We're only getting two of these because silver is a rare color, and I ordered these four months ago without much hope of getting any. Want to see it or drive it? Stop in on your way home today, Tuesday, because by tomorrow it might not still be here.

To a lesser extent, television offers a quick turnaround potential. But both broadcast media require acceptance and approval of your advertising message by the broadcaster. The Internet doesn't have to filter through a commercial manager and a continuity acceptance department. Want to change your message *right now*, before reading even the next paragraph? If you know the computer language and how to get to your site, what's stopping you?

But why would you want to change your message so frequently?

Two reasons: First, when people know they'll see something fresh, they're more likely to put your Internet address on their list of "Favorite Places" . . . which means a single mouse-click sends them to you.

Second, with the tens of thousands of sites and tens of millions of users, you don't want to risk having a potentially loyal visitor come back a couple of times and conclude there's nothing new.

That happens to big companies when Net exposure becomes a stepchild. Long after a major cellular phone company had merged itself into another company, there was its original site with its original name, sitting in solitary grandeur like a monument to bygone times.

Another company, a well-known clothing vendor, had "Father's Day Specials" still on sale in September.

Not all slow-changing offers are so blatantly out of tune with reality. But many (is yours one?) subordinate changes to day-to-day pressures in the office, and the result is the same decline in visitor interest an individual experiences at a trade show where speeches and exhibits are the same year after year.

Remember, as you structure your message: The Web is *different* from other media. Unless you pull the plug on your server, whatever you last put on it will be visible forever. Your mistakes are near-immortalized. That's not true of broadcast and it's not true of any print media. Billboards exhibit this behavior sometimes, when the billboard owner can't resell the space, but such occurrences are both rare and of fractional impact compared with the one-to-one impact of the Web.

Under some circumstances you can make immediate changes with no human intervention at all. That's when some of your content comes directly from a database. Quite a few sites now offer stock market quotations, either for a stored portfolio or as a simple query. The whole process can be automated through computer-to-computer communication, and you can provide up-to-the-minute information.

Don't limit yourself. If visitors to the Web want to obtain information stored in your corporate database, providing access to that information violates nobody's privacy and you have no plans to charge for that information . . . then you have the opportunity to say, "Click here to see ten new real-estate listings in YOUR neighborhood" and know as an absolute fact you're telling the truth.

# The Medium's Unique Strengths

In the early days of Internet marketing, sound and motion were rare for two reasons: Expense and lack of easy construction.

Too, not every computer had the guts and the memory to handle sound and motion. But more and more, as sophistication demands it, the Net finds itself in the same position television advertisers were in two generations ago—the necessary transition from still-slides to action. So the *avant-garde* marketers, recognizing that they had the technology (if you can digitize it you can present it), added sound and motion even though these additions were irritating to those who couldn't receive the messages in toto. Worse: They downloaded slowly.

Here we have another example of decision making: Do we want to be on the cutting edge or do we want to appeal to the broadest group of potential responders? For the typical marketer, the answer has to be broad response. Regrettable, yes . . . but sensible from a staying-in-business point of view.

Just be careful not to miss the great waves as they roll ashore.

One other advantage Internet marketers enjoy is the singular ability to test. A "Today only!" offer can change each day, and although no sane arbiter would suggest Tuesday and Saturday are parallel, a quick reading of results can dictate exposure in other, more expensive, media. You can also do A/B splits, by programming your Web server to present alternating pages to different visitors as they show up. As with all other one-to-one media, testing can be one of your most powerful tools.

History, a century from now, will judge the Internet on two levels: (1) How it advanced the techniques of communication and information or didn't advance the techniques of communication and information; (2) whether it became a major force, parallel to television, or a minor player, parallel to skywriting.

The unique strengths of the Net—its ability to implement quick changes and its interactivity—had better outbalance its unique weaknesses—the slowness of message-downloading and the bewildering superarray of competition for attention—if this medium is to be more than a curio.

# The Perfect Ancillary Medium

This may seem to be an oxymoron: One of the *primary* benefits the Internet offers a marketer is its availability as an *ancillary* or auxiliary medium.

A typical example of this use is a small section of a magazine advertisement by Intel, the computer chip maker:

For more information, contact your local PC dealer. Or you can dial our FaxBack number at 1-800-525-3019, doc. #8739; call 1-800-538-3373, ext. 296; or visit our Web site at http://www.intel.com/procs/ovrdrive/ to learn more.

Assuming you had a modem of reasonable speed, which would you choose? You *know* what happens when you call that toll-free number: You're locked in an electronic jungle: "Dial 1 if you want to wait less than half an hour. . . . " The Web site has a bunch of advantages:

- Page down quickly until you see what you're looking for, then print it.

- No waiting, except the usual Net delays to reach the site . . . usually far shorter delays than reaching a live person on the toll-free line.

- Unlimited information potential.

- Better print quality than fax-back, and your customers can store the information in a computer file if they prefer.

Note, please, that if you're using your Web site for ancillary information, you have to advertise the availability of the site elsewhere. That's why it's ancillary in the first place. But unloading technical tips and helpful hints onto a site has no limitations at all. If it's a thousand pages, it's a thousand pages.

The big advantage: This can be solid text, because *the site visitor is <u>looking</u> for text*. It doesn't have to be pretty, and gimmicking it up will damage its effectiveness.

From a business point of view, it frees not just technicians but telephone operators from many ties-up-the-lines calls, and it's the best of all possible worlds: The person asking for information is making a local call.

Consider using your site, or at least part of it, as a question-answering medium. You can make changes in minutes, so obsolescence is never a factor. It doesn't have to be pretty, so your art director can concentrate on more directly profitable advertising. And you'll win friends by having it on call 24 hours a day.

This use provides two separate benefits. First, you can satisfy research-oriented buyers far better than with any other medium by providing as much information, in as much depth, as each buyer wants. Second, you enhance relationships with current customers by providing a new level of customer service.

# Catalogs on the Net

A huge percentage of printed catalog sales comes from two sources:

1.  Those who chance upon the catalog, see something they like, and order;

2.  Those who, while ordering one item, page through the catalog and decide to order a second item totally unrelated to the first.

Both these advantages are "iffy" in the Internet because accessing the Internet more closely parallels response to classified advertising than response to any other technique of distant sale: The browser has to enter a key word. The process parallels looking for homes for sale or classic cars or office equipment in the classified pages. If the surfer is looking for a loft to rent and the Net marketer is offering a terrific bargain on Jeep Grand Cherokees, they'll never see each other.

That's why headings and greetings are crucial to not only the success of Internet catalogs but to their basic visibility.

## HOW DOES INTERNET CATALOG COPYWRITING DIFFER?

In theory—and, usually, in practice—Internet catalog copy doesn't differ at all from its paper cousins.

But this might be a mistake based on the oversimplified rationalization that a catalog is a catalog, in whatever medium it appears. It isn't, and this is why:

Let's suppose you're browsing or surfing or for that matter gawking. Are you truly in a buying mood? . . . Or are you enjoying the medium *as a medium?*

The gap between casual lookers and customers is ocean-wide in the world of printed catalogs and planet-wide in the universe of electronic catalogs. To convert an Internet surfer to a customer, shock treatment is in order, for two reasons:

1. Photographs not only aren't remotely as precise or crisp as those in a printed catalog, but . . .

2. In a printed catalog, one photograph and 50 photographs take the same time to present on a page. On the Internet, 50 photographs on a page will result in rapid movement away from your interminable download.

So enthusiasm has to permeate the copy. Here's Net copy for an attaché case, offered by a well-known cataloger. Note that it typifies copy in the *printed* catalog:

Lighthouse Attache

The Lighthouse Attache is our lightest and sportiest, yet it's still plenty tough. Made of rugged vinyl-backed nylon cloth, it weighs just 10 oz. We sew it with bound and welted seams that won't give out on you, and the fabric "gives," unlike hard-sided attaches. Whatever your line of work, its 10 almost infinitely adaptable interior pockets are sure to provide a place for most all your portable office needs. Its roomy exterior pocket has space for important last-minute files. Useful umbrella and key holders; carrying strap, luggage tag included. Made in USA. 17½" × 13½" × 3½".

Colors: Dark Burgundy, Black, Charcoal, Hunter, Classic Navy, Olive Khaki, Regal Navy.

SKU #2869-9M99

$42.50

Adequate? Certainly. But what if, for the Internet, the cataloger had offered a "Today only" or "This week only" $5.00 discount . . . provided (for phone-in orders) the consumer mentions a code number in this electronic version of the description?

What if the cataloger added a hyperlink that said, "If you want to know exactly how this attaché is put together, click here," where clicking leads to blueprints and exact dimensions. Nobody could afford to include this level of detail in a printed catalog, and doing so would make for an impossible layout. On the Internet it's a natural, and caters to the kind of intense information-seeking common in consumers buying products they intend to use for a long time.

Figure 8–2 shows a sophisticated cataloger's sophisticated use of the Web. Finding merchandise is actually easier than in this same marketer's printed catalogs. The text is largely a pickup from print. In this instance, because of the conversational tone of the original, copy alterations are minimal if made at all.

This catalog copy translates well to the Net because it's brisk and pointed. The cataloger who knows how to blend this with the personality of the Net is the one who develops an exciting new profit-center.

## PROS, CONS, AND CRYSTAL BALL

Because a catalog browser has to use a "mouse" to reveal copy longer than a handful of lines, and because illustrations aren't comparable to those in conventional printing processes, the Internet cataloger is best off promoting items that lean on (a) timeliness; (b) huge bargain; (c) quick availability; (d) closeouts; (e) extensive research prior to purchase.

# The Advantage of an Expiration Date

Direct marketers knew, long before the Internet was a gleam in the eye of its originators, the value of an expiration date.

In one short sentence:

**An expiration date improves response.**

The Net is a classic direct marketing medium. It's one-to-one, and it's far more personal and intimate than a bulk-mailed letter.

On the Net, an expiration date serves two purposes: First, it keeps the site *alive*. The parallel is one of the television shopping networks, which measure expiration not in days but in minutes and even seconds. Even the most jaded channel-hopper has to be fascinated by a digital clock ticking away in the lower right corner, narrowing and narrowing the amount of time left: Order or else!

Running out of time is the second purpose. The site visitor knows that the following hour or day or week, another offer will be in place. So the expiration date is a device that helps convince the visitor to come back again.

Tying the expiration date to what appears to be a singular offer gives that expiration date significance.

## CONCLUSION

Technically, ease of download is a major factor in tailoring your offers to the Net.

Saleswise, the overtone of "Special Offer!" . . . "Good only until midnight tonight!" . . . "Just three of these left" . . . "Available only through the Web" . . . this type of promotional copy exploits the medium as a medium. And exploiting the medium as a medium is what keeps visitors coming back.

**FIGURE 8–1**

*Not only does this page download quickly, but the information on the sample link—
even though far more extensive than one would expect for a single Cabernet Sauvignon—
is presented in an easy-to-read, easy-to-comprehend manner. Note "Ask the Cork Dork" on
the home page. Had this been called, "Answers to Your Logical Questions About Fine
Wines," unquestionably the number of "hits" would be reduced.*

## ** <u>Special Limited Offer</u> **

Virtual Vineyards helps you buy the same <u>specialty foods</u> & <u>excellent wines</u> that renowned wine expert
<u>Peter Granoff</u> recommends to his friends and family. Use Peter's <u>trademarked tasting chart</u> instead of
oversimplified numerical ratings to help you select wines that match *your* tastes. Using Virtual
Vineyards' <u>on-line order form</u> is the most convenient and <u>guaranteed</u> way to get these limited
production bottlings and specialty foods for yourself and as gifts.

<u>Peter's Quick Picks</u>        <u>Gift Packs to the Rescue</u>        <u>Better by the Case</u>

**A sparkling wine with a bubbly personality- <u>1990 Blanc de Blancs Brut!</u>**

<u>What's New</u> | <u>Monthly Wine Program</u> | <u>Specials</u> | <u>Ordering Fast Path</u> | <u>Personal Menu</u>

➥ Pick up Specialty <u>Food Convenience Packs</u> & <u>Wine Samplers.</u>

➥ Explore all [ <u>38</u> ] <u>Featured Wineries</u> and extensive <u>Wine Portfolio.</u>

➥ Enjoy everything in <u>The Cupboard</u> from our <u>Specialty Food</u> Producers.

➥ Pair <u>Food with Wine</u> & <u>Ask the Cork Dork.</u>

**P.S.** Peter's <u>Email List</u> is a great way to Stay Tuned into Virtual Vineyards.

<u>Quick Tour</u> | <u>Ordering, Security, & Privacy</u> | <u>Table of Contents</u> | <u>Questions?</u>

Copyright 1994, 1995 <u>Virtual Vineyards</u>. All logos, the Tasting Chart, product labels, company names,
and product names are service marks, trademarks, or registered trademarks belonging either to Virtual
Vineyards or to their respective companies and are used by permission. ALL RIGHTS RESERVED.

**FIGURE 8–2A**

*This Web catalog nicely bridges the gap between print and interactive electronics. Obviously, for a catalog the amount of "interactivity" usually has only two facets—finding merchandise and ordering it. Here, ordering is so easily step-by-step that unquestionably some who might be turned off by the usual catalog order forms will respond. Note, however, in Figure 8–2F, "From $64.00," unexplained on the page,* prevents *an order: a marketing mistake.*

## Where in the world can you find first-quality classic clothing and soft luggage at Direct Merchant prices?

**FIGURE 8–2B**

<u>Out our way...</u> we're passionate about creating comfortable clothing from nature's most essential fibers - the finest long staple cottons, Moygashel linens, first quality British woolens, the rarest of Mongolian cashmeres. Plus high performance fabrics Mother Nature never dreamed of. All crafted into timeless wardrobe classics at <u>Direct Merchant</u> prices. And all <u>Guaranteed. Period®.</u>

## <u>On-line Ordering</u> with <u>Netscape Navigator®</u> (NEW)

 **Dateline Dodgeville - January, 1996** (NEW)

 **The Goods**

 **Our Catalogs**

 **Services**

 **Gift Ideas**

 **Let's Talk**

 **The Company Inside and Out**

 **The Library**

**FIGURE 8–2C**

## Great Any-Time Gift ideas

**Find shopping a daunting experience?**

Here's a short list of easy to-fit, or no-fit gifts, including our specially-priced Laptop Computer Pouch and Computer Attache. Like five of our most popular <u>monogrammable gifts</u> we'll personalize to suit the giftee to a T, using your choice of our nine different monogramming styles. We've raised monogramming to a high art - at a reasonable cost - only $5.00 per item. So be sure to visit our full Internet Store... and check the list below for even more monongrammable gifts.

**All products (unless noted) are designed for both women and men.**

Just click on the item name and the product's presentation will appear. Then, make your pick (or choose any item in our Internet store as a gift), and we'll get it on its way! And for an additional $5.00 per gift, we'll gift box your selection, enclose your message on a gift card, and ship it directly (at the shipping mode/rate you select) to them - or to you - virtually anywhere in the world.

> <u>The Lands' End Gift Certificate</u>
>
> <u>Cobble Cloth Crew</u>
> <u>Shaker Sweater</u>
> <u>Men's Denim Sportshirt</u>
> <u>Polartec Jacket</u>
> <u>Women's Fine Gauge Sweater</u>
> <u>Leather Attache</u>

**Monogrammable Gifts (also available without monogram):**

> <u>Mesh Knit Shirt</u>
> <u>Women's Giant Sleep</u>
> <u>Terry Robe</u>
> <u>Portfolio</u>
> <u>Lighthouse Attache</u>
> <u>Original Attache</u>
> <u>Lighthouse Solo Voyager</u>

**FIGURE 8–2D**

Lighthouse Stowaway

**Great gifts for computer users at reduced prices:**

Computer Attache

**Can't decide which of these gifts is just right? Give the Lands' End Gift Certificate,** and let the person on whom you bestow it select the gift of their choice. We'll send our Gift Certificate with a free three-month subscription to our catalog, so they'll have a vast selection from which to choose. (Even picky people are bound to find something they'd enjoy.)

**Eager to order?**

Now you can send in your order directly from any Lands' End Internet store product page using our new On-line Ordering system. Or download our Electronic Order Blank program for Windows and use it at any time to send in an order for any item in any of our catalogs. If you prefer, you can also call toll-free (in the U.S. and Canada) 7 days a week, 24 hours a day at 1-800-963-4186; or, if you're calling from elsewhere in the world, please call (country code) 1-608-935-6170. Or fax your order to Lands' End at 1-800-332-0103 from the U.S. of Canada, or from all other countries, (country code) 1-608-935-4000. Fax orders can be placed with a credit card only. Happy shopping!

We hope this short cut makes your gift shopping just a little bit simpler, and that the selections you make win raves with the friends, family and colleagues who receive them. And with you, too.

Click here for five monogrammable gifts, that win raves year after year from our customers. And don't forget to visit our growing Internet Store!

**Check in often for more gift ideas and easy shopping solutions!**

December 22, 1995
Copyright © 1995 - Lands' End, Inc. Comments to mailbox@landsend.com

**FIGURE 8–2E**

## Looking for perfectly personalized gifts?
## Choose from our customers' five favorite monogrammable gifts.

Here are five of our most famous products that fit the bill. They've been perennially popular with our customers and are guaranteed to please just about anyone on your holiday shopping list. All are an "easy fit" (or in the case of our Original Attache, no fit at all), and are so well made that you and your gift are likely to be appreciated for many holiday seasons to come.

<u>Men's Oxford Shirt</u>
<u>Men's and Women's Turtleneck</u>
<u>Men's and Women's Drifter(TM) Sweaters</u>
<u>Men's and Women's Terry Robe</u>
<u>Original Attache</u>

**How to make them uniquely personal?**

Add a monogram in any of our nine <u>monogramming styles</u>. You can have their initials, name, or a nickname of up to 10 characters monogrammed. (One we suggest for Internet aficionados is their e-mail "name" ending with an @ sign, or @ + their e-mail "location.") Naturally, you can order any of these products without the monogram, too.

**Want to send it directly?**

We'll even wrap your gift in a handsome <u>Gift Box</u> and add a message in your own words for an additional $5.00 per gift, then send it on its way - nearly anywhere in the world. (Shipping is additional, of course.)

**Eager to order?**

Now you can send in your order directly from any Lands' End Internet store product page using our new <u>On-line Ordering</u> system. Or download our <u>Electronic Order Blank</u> program for Windows and use it at any time to send in an order for any item in any of our catalogs. If you prefer, you can also call toll-free (in the U.S. and Canada) 7 days a week, 24 hours a day at 1-800-963-4186; or, if you're calling from elsewhere in the world, please call (country code) 1-608-935-6170. Or fax your order to Lands' End at 1-800-332-0103 from the U.S. of Canada, or from all other countries, (country code) 1-608-935-4000. Fax orders can be placed with a credit card only. Happy shopping!

We hope this short cut makes your gift shopping just a little bit simpler, and that the selections you make win raves with the friends, family and colleagues who receive them. And with you, too.

**FIGURE 8–2F**

 **Internet Store**

# Men's and Women's Terry Robe

**From $64.00**

## It happens to everyone.

It never fails. The phone always rings when you're getting out of the shower. Letting the answering machine pick it up would be way too easy. Instead, you make a mad dash for the phone, stubbing your toe along the way, no doubt, trying to get there before it stops ringing.

Of course, the same thing always happens. You wind up standing there naked, dripping wet, while the person on the other end rambles on about switching your long-distance company. (Ever think of investing in a robe? It might be a little less embarrassing if video phones ever hit it big.)

Finding a robe that fits isn't as easy as you might think. Most are one size fits all. Not quite. You're either left overexposed or with too much hanging around. Ours come in individual sizes for men and women to cover up this problem. (Both are mid-calf, but the women's also comes in full length for total coverage.) Larger armholes give you plenty of room to stretch, too.

We don't use flimsy cotton terry either. (The kind that wears so thin you can practically see through it.) No way. It's the thick 14 oz. stuff for us. We loop it on both sides too. Gives it twice the drying power.

Some robes get tattered and torn over time. To prevent this we put heavy-duty stitching (double-needle stitching, actually) at the shoulders and sleeve seams to keep them from ripping or fraying.

# 9 Presentation— Design and Layout on the Web

Most marketers have come to the same, reluctant conclusion: the tie between artistic layout and sales power is tenuous at best. That's fortunate for Web-based marketers (and unfortunate for designers posing as marketers), since the Web gives you only imperfect control over page design anyway.

In this chapter we'll cover what you can do, what you can't do, and what you probably should do. We'll also do a bit of crystal-ball gazing and try to give you some idea of what you'll be able to do in the future as the technology evolves.

Don't worry! We're not going to force you through a primer on the Hypertext Markup Language. You may want to review some of the technobabble in Chapter One, so you have a reasonable understanding of how the medium works.

The key word in putting Web pages together is "tradeoff." You have several.

- You can take advantage of layout features only Netscape can present (at press time), such as tables. Tradeoff: your page looks better on Netscape's browser but worse on all others.

- You can transmit elegant graphics and digitized photographs to dress up your page. Tradeoff: your page will take so long to transmit you'll lose half your potential following.

- You can achieve almost perfect control over the appearance of your Web pages by putting everything inside an embedded graphic image—an "interactive graphic." Tradeoff: your download has become longer yet.

- You can manage page transmission time by breaking your site down into more, smaller linked pages. Tradeoff: visitors can't do a quick scan of your site.

- You can compress photographic images more to reduce transmission time. Tradeoff: the pictures don't look as good.

- You can use line art and other forms of computer-generated graphic instead of photographs wherever possible to reduce picture size. Tradeoff: drawings rarely have the impact of photographs.

You can find dozens of good books on HTML at any store with a computer section. The HTML specification is evolving at a pace that would make any specifics provided here obsolete long before you can buy this book. And since you (as a creative source, not a "techie") won't have to deal with the details of HTML coding anyway—lots of products have appeared that automate the details for you—this book shouldn't and won't go into detail regarding design aesthetics and how to achieve graphic nirvana on the Web.

Instead, some basic practical advice.

Many standard presentation guidelines for conventional print media parallel those of good Web copy. Others are complementary. Some depend on context, others make sense everywhere. As a generalization, this isn't much help to the about-to-be-creator, fingers poised on the computer keys. As a specific—*If it grabs and holds the eye in print media it's a good <u>start</u> on the Web*—it's almost universally applicable.

The First Rule of Internet Advertising will never fail you:

**Stop the surfer in his/her tracks.**

Then what? Let's marry the creative with the technical. (A shotgun wedding? A necessary pill for both parties . . . and many shotgun weddings result in beautiful issues.)

# Universal Guidelines

The Web has some frustrating characteristics for page designers. Learn to live in harmony with those characteristics since you can't do anything about them anyway.

For example:

- You have no control over how much fits onto a single computer screen. Objects displayed under 640 × 480 resolution take up much more screen real-estate than objects displayed under 1024 × 768 resolution.

- Depending on how much time and care you want to apply to the problem, you can either decide what you consider the minimum configuration to be and design for it (800 × 600 is a good compromise as of this writing), or you can test your design using several different resolutions and tune it to the best compromise you can.

- You can't control color depth, either. Windows users operate under 16-color palettes, 256-color palettes, and 16-million-color palettes. Again, either pick a minimum configuration or test a bunch of different ones. As of this writing, 256 colors is a good choice if you have to pick one.

- You can't control font size. Depending on the Web browser, the *end-user* can control at least the size of all fonts, and possibly the choice of each font used for every single HTML code.

- And of course, not only do different Web browsers display the same HTML codes differently. Most non-Netscape browsers can't handle Netscape enhancements, such as tables.

## More Problems than Solutions

Okay, those are problems. Do any solutions exist, or at least some helpers for the frustrated Web marketer? Yes, some do:

- Organize your Web site into a branching tree that starts with your home page and branches out into subsection headers (home pages for subsections of your site), fact pages, narratives, forms, thumbnail galleries, pictures, link pages and so on. These are generic descriptions—you don't have to be rigid. Your hierarchy doesn't have to be rigid either. You can help visitors reach important pages by as many different paths as makes sense.

- As a general rule, keep your layouts uncomplicated, and focus on the contents of each page element rather than trying to achieve complicated element positioning. (As we've said so often in this text, attention to form instead of substance is a killer in any medium.)

Here are five universal "helpers" to prevent not only disasters but early departure by disgusted surfers:

**1. An obvious basic: Include your corporate logo at the top of every page in your Web site.**

If you've organized your site into products, also put a product logo at the top when it makes sense.

*Of Vital Importance:* Minimize the file size of your logo. Don't let ego overcome common sense, which is a standard precursor to the attitudinal flaw of valuing form over substance. Have your logo float over a background and compress it 'til it hurts. You're best off if you can get it to 5K or smaller. Also, tell your "techie" (or your fingers) to make it an embedded graphic so each page points to the same logo file. Why? Most browsers will store it locally after the first download (they *cache* it, to use the technical term) so it will display much faster on every subsequent page.

### 2. Never create a page sub-element that spreads beyond a single computer screen.

It doesn't matter how well it prints. The Web is interactive, and if a visitor has to scroll back and forth to see the whole image, you've diluted the impact of your message beyond salvage.

### 3. Use "Image Maps" for impact, but don't overdo it.

The term *image maps* refers to any graphic image which responds to a mouse click in different ways, depending on where in the image you click. For example, clicking on Delaware in a weather map of the United States might bring up the weather for Delaware.

### 4. No matter how attractive your graphics and image maps may be, also include text versions of all links.

That way, visitors don't have to wait for your graphics to finish downloading.

### 5. Code your pages so that text displays before graphics start to download.

Why? Because your visitor still feels he or she is being interactive. Long waits parallel watching the meter of a taxicab build up a fare while the cab is stopped in traffic.

One other note: *Every* page should include a top-level directory to your site; and except for the home page itself, every page should have a link back to the home page. A common style (and a good one): put a graphical version of the directory at the top of each page, and a text version at the bottom along with the home page link.

# Home Page Guidelines

Your home page has a host of different responsibilities. You won't find any easy formula for balancing them. Here they are:

1. *Introduce your site:* After a quick read of your home page, visitors will want to understand what you're trying to accomplish. Clarity reigns as the preeminent virtue here. If you don't know what you're trying to accomplish, nobody else will either. And if your whole goal is to be cool . . . good luck. Being cool is—well, it's cool—but those who appreciate coolness aren't those who are most likely to buy anything.

2. *Grab their attention:* See Chapter Five for specifics. To repeat it for emphasis here—you **absolutely must** have a grabber on your home page. It should be evident above the monitor cutoff line, even at 640 × 480 resolution, and it must be presented in text-only form. Presence in the graphic is optional.

3. *Serve as Table of Contents:* You have their attention and you've made clear what your site is for. Your home page, by definition, provides links to the rest of your site. Make those links clear and concise, but not dull. If you can't fit a

table of contents on your home page, put it on a separate page and design your home page with a prominent link to it.

4. *Point to the New Stuff:* You should have a constant stream of new material. Make it easy for repeat visitors to find. Two easy approaches: either put a "New Stuff" item in the contents list, or create a "New" bug (a tiny graphic, that is) and place it after every item less than a week old.

5. *Download Quickly:* The temptation to provide a gorgeous, full-color, full-page photograph with dozens of "hot spots" to click may be overwhelming, and the resulting page may in fact be a thing of beauty to behold.

   Regrettably, only a small fraction of your initial audience will wait long enough to find out.

   Think minimalist. Content goes on other pages, where you have more room to play. Remember, you have maybe five seconds to grab each visitor's attention. With a 14.4Kbps or 28.8Kbps modem (the most common types in use as of this writing) that means enough content has to appear in the first 7,000 bytes or so to keep them there for the rest. You're subject to a *double* caution: Not only might your slow download lose your surfer/potential visitor, but once that individual concludes your site is a slowpoke, it will be a long time, if ever, before he/she returns.

Home page design has a lot in common with magazine cover or book jacket design. As safe guidelines, with a 14.4Kbps modem text should appear within five seconds, the entire page should download within 15 seconds—20 at the outside, a "grabber" should appear within monitor boundaries, and the entire home page should print onto a single 8½" × 11" sheet of paper.

Don't let fear of slow downloading lead you into The Primitive Trap, such as Figure 9–1 exemplifies. If your home page looks home-made, image—or *lack* of image—overrides all favorable reaction.

# Subsection Headers Guidelines

Many of the pages in your Web site serve as second-level home pages. In other words, they serve the same function for subsections of your site as your home page does for the whole site. The rules are exactly the same as for the home page itself, with the addition of a link back to the Home Page.

Figures 9–2 and 9–3, for two automobile manufacturers, exemplify the ongoing "home page" look.

In Figure 9–2 for Ford, links appear everywhere, and most have a home page look. The surfer is given a tremendous number of options, from visiting the Jaguar Historical Library to filling out a "brief survey" (database development!) and becoming a member of the "World Wide Web Customer Focus Team." Pages for all these different elements have a fresh-start look.

In Figure 9–3 for General Motors, the lineup of brands gives the visitor a quick-look index for easy browsing. The quotation on the home page isn't particularly inspiring—in fact, it's a bit weak—but notice the Net-specific structure of the Saturn pages.

In some cases you may choose to cross-promote some of your subsection headers as well as your home page. This will make a lot of sense when you organize your site by product or product category. Include the URL for the product page in ads for that product.

# Fact Pages

The slow speed of the Web encourages quick presentation of summary information. Bulleted copy, tables, and quick, clear offers make a lot of sense in this medium.

Especially when you're catering to information seekers, make liberal use of this kind of page.

**But don't forget, ever: This book is titled "Selling on the Net"
and you wouldn't be reading it if getting response weren't your**

primary goal. Transmission of information has to be tied to cunning salesmanship or you're either in the wrong medium or operating the wrong kind of organization.

Resist the temptation to intersperse lots of pretty pictures into your Fact Pages. Pictures slow things down. Also resist the temptation to create run-on lists. Hold it to what will print on a single 8½" × 11" page, or at most two.

If you're willing to cater to Netscape and Microsoft Explorer users at the expense of the rest of the market (at this writing that's over 80 percent combined market share) use tables to create two-column lists whenever possible. This improves overall use of page real-estate.

# Narratives

Here's where you can present a lot of information. Write paragraphs. Write an essay. Illustrate it with pictures. It's okay—just don't go completely overboard.

No, you don't suddenly get complete control of your layout. In fact, you have all the fine control you'd use writing an interoffice memo. You can change font size, and you can get the equivalent of boldface, italic, and underscored text as well, although that's not what it's called when you use HTML.

You can include line drawings, graphs, and scanned photographs. You can include tabular information, if you're willing to expend a bit of effort.

But you *can't* create an on-screen newspaper with multiple columns. This medium is one story at a time. In the logic of the Web, that makes sense. Instead of multi-column formats, you have multiple links on a page.

Are you wondering . . .

Why is a long download suddenly okay when you're presenting a boatload of information? Because now you're providing extensive, detailed data. For the information seeker, the alternative would be a telephone call followed by a faxed response, or maybe a trip to the library. A two-minute wait is nothing compared to the alternatives.

A suggestion, rarely followed: *Invite* visitors to print these pages or save them to a file. With a little testing, you may even manage a color combination that reads clearly on-screen but prints out blank, so your invitation to print doesn't appear on the hard copy.

# Forms

HTML includes a primitive form-building ability. It doesn't have the sophistication you'd find in a PC database package: All you can do is provide a "blank" that accepts a bunch of typing, generate drop-down lists of legal entries for some fields, and provide button-click selections. That means a bunch of back-end programming to validate the entries, because when you ask for a telephone number your visitor could type *aV%4TEJLi89*. You can't force an accurate entry, but you want to make sure you reject unusable information.

Forms are Good Things (to use the technical term). They encourage interaction. They tell visitors you're interested in them. Don't be surprised that in today's age of sophisticated, skeptical customers, they also shout from the rooftops your desire to capture a visitor's identity and add it to your database. Visitors don't like to be "conned." Simple: Don't con them.

The easy, obvious, and ethical solution: ask permission. Put a check box next to the text, "May we add you to our preferred list (*not "database"*) of sophisticated consumers who want to know more about our products?" Put another one next to, "Shall we make your name available to a few, carefully selected providers of related products and services?"

Forms have other uses too, of course. You can use them to accept entries for trivia contests and other games, a universally accepted technique for name-gathering. If you want to be "retro," you can hold a jingle contest. Create a chat area for real interaction.

A related approach: use forms as an alternative to providing an e-mail address for your visitors to send you comments. (You should always use "Webmaster@yourcompany.com" as your e-mail address. It's *tradition*. In this context, that means it shows you know how things are done on the Web.)

Finally, you can use forms to let visitors order merchandise. As of this writing the most popular approach uses a shopping-cart metaphor. Each page displaying an item available for purchase includes the unit price and an entry area in which the visitor can key in how many should go into the "cart." The system keeps track of everything.

At the bottom of every page is a link to the ordering page, which accepts delivery and credit card information and displays a completed order form based on what went into the shopping cart.

# Thumbnail Galleries

Nothing to this one. You display a bunch of postage-stamp-size images on a page. Visitors click on the desired image and get a high-resolution full-screen version suitable for downloading or printing.

Why? You can compress thumbnails to between 5K and 10K, where the full image would occupy between 45K and 100K or more. That means a gallery of ten images will download as fast as just one high-resolution full-screen image.

Put a text link as a caption to each thumbnail, so impatient visitors can get right to the pictures they want, and say how big the file will be in each caption.

Strictly speaking, a thumbnail is a highly compressed, low-resolution version of an image that's also available in a higher-resolution equivalent. Sometimes (for example, in a catalog) you may be better off using small line-drawings in place of true thumbnails.

Why? Speed. People like to browse catalogs. Browsing requires fast rendering of each page. That means very small data volumes, which in turn means even a thumbnail version of a photograph is too much.

# Pictures

Visitors may want to download a picture for a variety of reasons. It may be an assembly diagram for a gadget they bought from you. It may be poster art they want as Windows Wallpaper (the background image on their computer screen). It may be a cartoon they can print on their new color ink-jet printer for their kids (these have now become inexpensive enough to be a consumer item).

You may show photographs of your merchandise, as many on-line catalogs do. You can show your wares nicely on a computer screen, if visitors will wait for the download.

Visitors may just want to admire a picture for the sheer novelty of it . . . or read it if it's a cartoon.

The most important rule for displaying pictures: Let visitors know how big the file is before they start to download it. Even a large download is acceptable under those circumstances, because your visitors can start the process and walk away from their computers while the download happens. Another alternative: Make downloading the picture an option.

# Links

Lots of Web sites provide a Link page, a directory of other useful, interesting or related Web sites. If you choose to do this, or to provide links in appropriate places throughout your Web site, make sure you understand why you're doing so.

The layout is easy: just use a bulleted list and have done with it. You're pointing to other sites, not your own, so you don't have to be very fussy.

When you provide a link to another site, it's as if you've installed a side door out of your store and into a different one. Think about the circumstances that would warrant such unusual architecture.

If you and the other merchant have a reciprocal agreement, this may make sense: New customers will enter through the same door.

If it means more visitors to your store because it's easier to reach other stores by walking past your merchandise, this may make sense too. It's the difference between being in a shopping mall and having a stand-alone store adjacent to nothing but a parking lot.

But if it just means people will remember that you provide a Link page . . . bad news. You don't want them to remember you as a link provider. You want them to remember you as selling something they want.

And if you do it just to prove you're cool, *watch out!* You probably haven't developed a solid business model for creating your Web site in the first place.

# Ignore This Chapter!

Not really. On the other hand, don't bind yourself slavishly to its advice, either. Marketing is a creative activity. Blind adherence to any set of rules will stifle your ability to innovate, and the Web is too new and changing a medium for that to be a good way to succeed.

If you make a single note, it should be this: Those who are more interested in the technique of Web page construction than they are in creating attractive, enticing offers are those who are least likely to use the Web profitably.

**FIGURE 9–1**

*What's the point of this page? It transmits no information, builds no desire to continue, and looks as though it were an afterthought. A job-seeker might be interested in these names, but a potential listener is more interested in the programming. After seeing this, the reaction might be: a group of semi-pros.*

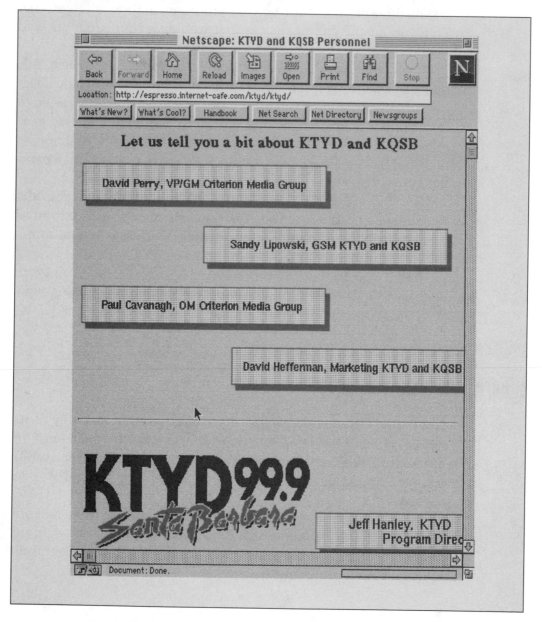

**FIGURE 9–2A**

*Links appear everywhere in this exposition. And most links have a fresh "home page" look. Notice the tremendous number of options, from visiting the Jaguar Historical Library to filling out a "brief survey" (database acquisition!) and becoming a member of the "World Wide Web Customer Focus Team." Pages for the model F-150 and the Customer Focus Team have a fresh-start look. The "Brief Survey" has 16 questions—including some personal ones, such as household income—with no indication of reward, a possible response suppressor.*

View the  1997 F150 Series

Take a drive down Showroom Boulevard. Visit the Ford, Mercury, Lincoln, and Jaguar showrooms and view model line profiles and auto specs for all of our 1996 models. When you're ready to try some out, use our Dealer Locator to find the dealer nearest you.

Ford is among the largest providers of financial services in the world. Discover the wide range of products and services available from the Ford Financial Services Group through its three businesses: Ford Credit, The Associates, and USL Capital.

Get the latest Ford Info. You can read Ford Chairman Alex Trotman's Personal Welcome, view or download current Stockholder Relations information, see what Ford is doing to help protect the Environment, and get the latest information about What's New at Ford from our Ford News Briefs weekly digest and in Jaguar Jottings. You can also catch a glimpse of our international divisions in Ford Around the World.

Visit the Ford Historical Library **and** the new Jaguar Historical Library in our **new expanded historical section!** Browse the archives to get the Ford Story as well as historical information about the Ford family's involvement in the company. Here too is where you will be able to find interesting information about classic cars.

Forge a Customer Link with Ford. Fill out a brief survey and join our World Wide Web Customer Focus Team. As a member of the team, you could be asked to review and critique some of our new product ideas and designs from time to time.

webmaster@www.ford.com

**FIGURE 9–2B**

# STRENGTH AFTER STRENGTH.

# THE ALL-NEW 1997 FORD F-150.

After 19 years of building America's best-selling truck, we're coming out with an all-new Ford F-Series: the 1997 F-150. It's longer. It has a wider stance. A taller cab. More power and V-8 payload than ever before. More safety and convenience features, too. And the new F-150 was put through more than 5-million miles torturous testing, so you know it's tough!

 **Strength After Strength**  **Comparisons** **Specifications/Prices**

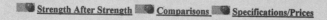

FORD CONNECTION    FORD SHOWROOM    DEALER LOCATOR

**FIGURE 9–2C**

## FORD CUSTOMER LINK: LINK UP WITH US!

Thanks for your interest in Ford! We want to provide you with the best vehicles and services in the world, but to do that we need to hear from you, our worldwide customers. We would like to know more about your needs and expectations, so we're inviting you to become a member of the **Ford World Wide Web Customer Focus Team** . To become a part of the team, just answer the questions below. Your answers will help us determine your areas of interest as they pertain to new products and special projects we are working on.

### HERE'S HOW IT WORKS:

Fill out the questionnaire below and include your e-mail address (all information you provide us will be kept strictly confidential). When you are finished, just click on **Register** and you will be registered as an "on-call" team member.

When we are ready for customer feedback on a product, service, or idea, we will search the file for a profile which matches the potential customer. If yours is a match, we will contact you via the e-mail address you provided, to request your participation. At that time, you can choose whether you want to participate or not. Ready?

1.  **Please describe the vehicle you currently drive:**

    Year:
    Make:
    Model:

2.  **How did you acquire this vehicle?**

    Financed  Leased  Cash

3.  **Do you drive frequently under the following conditions?**

**FIGURE 9–2D**

*(Please check all that apply.)*

Severe dust
Stop-and-go traffic in hot weather
Below freezing temperatures
Towing a trailer, boat, etc.
Mostly short trips (10 miles or less)

4.  **Where do you go for major repairs?**

Original dealership
Different dealership
Do it yourself
Specialty repair shops
Independent garage

5.  **Where do you go for routine service (oil changes, tune-ups, etc.)?**

Original dealership
Different dealership
Do it yourself
Specialty repair shops
Independent garage

6.  **How many miles do you generally drive in a month?**

7.  **How long do you expect to keep your current vehicle?**

8.  **How many vehicles are in your household?**

One  Two  Three  Four  Five or more

9.  **Of your total household vehicles, how many are Ford Motor Company vehicles?**

One  Two  Three  Four  Five or more  None

10.  **When do you plan to acquire your next vehicle?**

**FIGURE 9–3A**
*The lineup of automobile brands along the left edge gives the visitor a quick index from which to choose. The quotation on the home page isn't particularly memorable . . . and is, in fact, a weak introduction. But notice the Net-specific structure of "The 1996 Saturn Site" and "1996 Saturn Line" pages.*

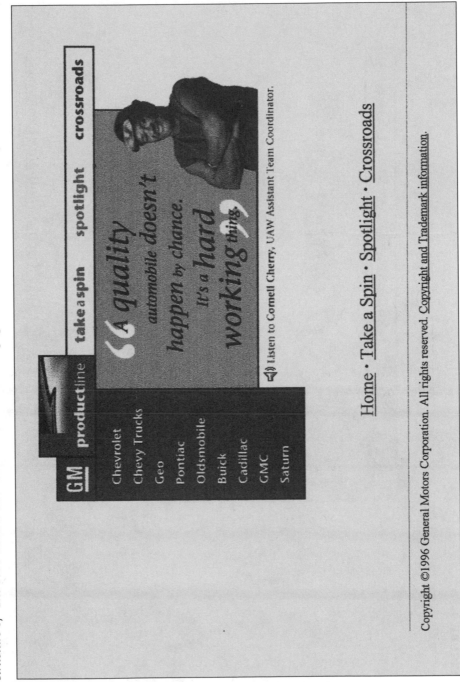

**FIGURE 9–3B**

**FIGURE 9–3C**

## Welcome to the Saturn Site!

We've designed this Website to help you find out all about Saturn, on your own, as easily as possible. So have fun exploring -- and if you still have questions, give us a call at 1-800-522-5000.

This site was launched in February, 1995, and updated for <u>Model Year 1996</u> in August, 1995. Check out these additional updates: In November, <u>Saturn Cycling Team</u> results were updated, and in December, information about the <u>Saturn CarClub</u> was added. During the past few months, a few retailers have developed their own sites, and we've linked them to the Saturn Site. And the Saturn <u>Extended Family Database</u> continues to grow.

And in January, we added some extra news: Saturn was selected to sell and service <u>General Motors' new electric car</u> (and we're pretty darn excited).

 <u>Welcome</u> (updated 8/95)

 <u>The 1996 Saturn Line</u> (updated 8/95)

 <u>The Saturn Magazine</u> (updated 12/95)

 <u>Find the Nearest Saturn Retailer</u> (updated 8/95)

 <u>Order a Saturn Brochure</u>

 <u>Communicate with Saturn</u> (updated 7/95)

 <u>Extended Family Database</u> (updated regularly)

 <u>Frequently Asked Questions</u> (updated 7/95)

**FIGURE 9–3D**

# The 1996 Saturn Line

Most visitors to the Saturn Site, we've found, are primarily interested in the same thing: a good look at our new 1996 line of cars. So, for your perusing pleasure, here's a page for each model with all the facts: features, options, and available accessories; colors, fabrics, specs and fine print; and photos from a couple of different angles.

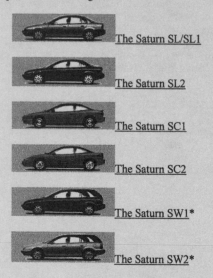

The Saturn SL/SL1

The Saturn SL2

The Saturn SC1

The Saturn SC2

The Saturn SW1*

The Saturn SW2*

*Available Spring, 1996

Home | Welcome | Cars | Magazine | Retailers | Brochure | Communicate | Database | FAQ

# 10 Commerce on the Internet

You've grabbed their attention. You've provided information, edutainment, free stuff with a tie-in to your real merchandise. They've played your games, entered your contests, and admired your graphics.

They're ready to buy. Now what?

Now you let them.

One of the marvels of twentieth-century America is the number of companies that make the process of buying hard. Hard-to-find sales clerks, hard-to-understand order forms, understaffed call centers, well-hidden toll-free numbers, bewildering pricing options—it's a long list.

If there's one rule of business that has to outweigh all others in terms of importance, it's this: when a customer wants to give you money, *TAKE IT RIGHT AWAY*. Don't provide any opportunities for second thoughts.

The Internet gives you wonderful tools to make it really, really easy for customers to buy from you. Take advantage of them. That's what this chapter is about.

You have two problems to solve in helping customers buy from you: making it easy for them to tell you what they want, and making it both secure and convenient to pay you. We'll take these one at a time.

# Taking Orders on the Web

Let's begin with a straightforward Web-based business that describes a variety of merchandise available for purchase and immediate shipment. Call it an on-line catalog.

You could handle this the same way you'd manage it in a printed catalog, providing an order form on a separate page. Customers would enter catalog numbers and quantities in the form, pressing the "SUBMIT" button when they're done.

You could do it this way, but it would be, shall we say, suboptimal. That's a euphemism for "dumb."

Don't make your customers write down catalog numbers on scraps of paper, or page back and forth. Instead, use a shopping cart approach.

Every place you describe an item, include its price, provide a place for customers to enter a quantity, and add a pushbutton labeled "Add to Shopping Cart." Damark's home page (Figure 10–1) demonstrates this technique.

At the bottom of every page make sure you have a button labeled "Place Order."

The "Place Order" button links to a page that presents a filled-out order form and places to enter customer name and address and payment information (covered later in this chapter).

A nicety here: always display item extensions (quantities times unit prices) and the current total order. This takes no effort at all on your part, and doing it separates the professionals from the amateurs.

A second nicety: tell customers when to expect delivery. At a minimum, provide your standard shipment policy. Better: link your Web site to your order-processing and inventory databases, and let customers know when they've ordered out-of-stock items. Of course, what you <u>really</u> do is display a cheery "In Stock! 24 Hour Shipping Guaranteed!" bug after each item you do have.

A third, obvious, nicety: let customers choose from a menu of shipment methods. Make sure your totals include shipping costs, and sales tax if that's appropriate.

A fourth nicety which also should be obvious: give Web customers a special discount, display the calculated discount prominently on the order form, and display both the undiscounted total and your customer's special price. It's less important to do this for each item than it is for the whole order. You want to say, "Regular Order Amount" and "Your Special Discounted Amount" on the order form.

Nice and simple. Just make sure you have plenty of processing power behind your Web site, so customers don't have to wait every time they press the "Add to Shopping Cart" button. Remember, *Waiting is a Bad Thing* (to use technical terms).

It's your good fortune this isn't a technical book. The shopping cart interface is easy to describe. Programming it takes some work. Lucky for you someone else will have to handle the tricky parts.

If you sell only a small number of products, you can create a check-off order form instead of creating a shopping cart. Figures 10–2 and 10–3 show how two different beer-of-the-month clubs use this approach—Red White and Brew (Figure 10–2) and The Great American Beer Club (Figure 10–3). Both offer simple forms to fill out. The tactic works in these cases because the clubs have just one product. (Note: the printed versions of these forms don't show the entry fields and check-boxes as effectively as they're shown on-screen, where they're obvious and easy to interpret.)

Figure 10–4 shows an order form used on the Brothers' Coffee site. This is exactly the wrong approach to use: the only way customers will be able to remember Item Numbers from elsewhere on the site would be to scrawl them down on a piece of paper to later re-enter them on the form. *Ease of ordering* is a crucial factor that can be a Web site advantage or a Web site liability. Why make customers do the work of the computer?

# Taking Orders on the Phone

Lots of people just plain don't trust computers. It's hard to figure out exactly why. Computers, after all, never make mistakes.

Still, hard as it may be to believe, some of your customers may be among those people who don't trust computers. Make it easy for them to order, too. How?

The same way you cater to customers who don't like to fill out forms and lick postage stamps: print a toll-free number on every Web page. Obviously, it should be a unique number so you can track the effectiveness of your site. Less obviously, you need to make a hard decision regarding discounts. An opinion: you should offer a smaller discount for telephone orders.

A company called *Spanlink* (http://www.spanlink.com) has a product that lets you split the difference. Called *WebCall*, it lets customers click on an icon and enter their telephone number. It inserts them into your call center's automated call distributor (ACD) queue and automatically calls them when the next agent is available, after advising them on how long that's likely to be.

If you want to be fancy, you can link it into your order-processing system so your call center agent sees a filled-out order before ever talking to your customer.

Psychologically, many people simply want to talk to a human being when buying. (As a point of reference, 1995 was the first year more than half of all banking customers were willing to use Automated Teller Machines. And lots of them still won't use the machines for deposits.)

The L.L. Bean site, as of press time, not only emphasizes telephone ordering through a toll-free number (Figure 10–5), it turns its lack of on-line ordering into a virtue. Expressing its concern over security, it instead provides a toll-free number, along with a cumbersome-to-use downloadable order form suitable for faxing or mailing. Disingenuous or sincere, L.L. Bean avoids the cost of creating a secure transaction environment while sidestepping any negative customer reaction.

# For More Information ...

Not all products and services lend themselves to on-line ordering. Expensive offerings, complicated products and services, or items requiring extensive customization, all will require more customer handling before closing a sale.

This doesn't invalidate use of the Web as part of your selling process. Quite the contrary. You can use the Web to provide huge amounts of product information, screening out casual browsers from qualified leads at a very low cost.

Okay, now what?

Simple: offer a toll-free number to speak with a "consultant." Use *WebCall* if you like that approach, give your e-mail address (you *do* have an e-mail address, don't you? Remember, Web tradition suggests the address *Webmaster@your company.com.*), or . . . provide an on-screen form.

On that form, ask for as much information as you need to understand who should call the prospect back, but not so much as to be annoying. Name, address, and telephone number make sense. So does a fax number and e-mail address. Ask what products or services your prospect wants more information about. Ask when calls are convenient. Stop there.

When your prospect presses the "Submit" button, *say when you'll call back.* It's a minor courtesy, but an important one.

Many sites, in a misguided attempt to be helpful, provide a hypertext link to electronic mail. In theory, this should work well—bring up your visitor's e-mail system with a send-mail form ready to go.

In practice, regrettably, many of your visitors won't have their browsers configured to make this option work well. The most common reason: They use an unlinkable e-mail system like Microsoft Mail, Lotus cc:Mail, or Novell Groupwise as their regular system.

Fortunately, you have an easy alternative: just create a simple entry form with three fields: their name, e-mail address, and message. You can store this information in a database, or have your

Web server mail each message to you. The only thing you lose: Visitors may choose to avoid giving you their e-mail address.

# Accepting Payment

Here's where life gets complicated. You have a confusing array of options, consumer distrust based on hysterical reporting about computer hackers, and few success stories to guide you.

You can transact business over the Internet with confidence, though. Here are your best options. Regardless of the option you choose, follow one key rule: don't store any sensitive information on your Web server. The simplest and safest approach uses what's called an "airgap firewall," which simply means you never connect your Web server to your internal network at the same time it's connected to the Internet. Instead you store transactions in temporary files and use a simple file transfer to relay them to your internal systems. Engage a security expert to engineer the details.

Your options and their respective advantages follow.

## HOUSE ACCOUNTS

Here's a simple, safe, secure, reliable and trustworthy way to let customers buy from you on the Web. Let customers establish credit accounts with your company, either in person or over the telephone. Use whatever techniques you prefer to verify the information. Use their home phone number as an account number. Or, if it makes sense in the context of your business, give them a personal identification number (PIN) and use it in conjunction with their phone number.

Customers can order over the Internet with confidence. Why would anyone bother hacking their PIN when you'll ship all merchandise to the address in your database anyway?

The key advantage of this approach: its simplicity. The biggest disadvantage: you lose impulse buyers and visitors who haven't yet established a relationship with you. The act of setting up a credit account represents a sales barrier, especially for many common consumer activities. This approach will work best with stable business-to-business relationships, although some consumer situations may lend themselves to it as well.

## ENCRYPTED TRANSACTIONS

Several software suppliers, most notably Netscape, have developed technology that encrypts business transactions before sending them over the Internet. Because they use hard-to-crack encryption techniques, credit card information should be safe from prying hackers.

Lurid commentary from the press to the contrary, the encryption techniques used in these programs are more than good enough for consumer transactions and most business-to-business use. A well-publicized "hole" in Netscape's security—since fixed— took nine days of computing time on high-speed computers to crack. Who's going to bother with this kind of computer theft? Nine days to get a single credit card? It's easier to steal the carbons at a restaurant.

According to First Virtual, a company offering competing technology, these techniques are also vulnerable to a different line of attack, called a "keyboard sniffer." This is a program inserted into customers' computers without their knowledge. The program watches everything typed into the computer, looking for credit card numbers, which are easy to recognize.

When it finds a credit card number, it automatically sends the number to a crook over the Internet next time the user goes online. Since sniffers see credit card numbers before they're encrypted, they bypass the whole elaborate security scheme.

First Virtual says there's no defense against keyboard sniffers, which aren't, by the way, viruses. They're a related critter called a "Trojan Horse" . . . for obvious reasons. Actually, it shouldn't be all that difficult to add a sniffer-detector to existing anti-virus programs, and it also may be possible to add a monitor program that watches for transmission of unencrypted credit card numbers and blocks them.

That's the nature of security: measure, countermeasure, counter-countermeasure, and so forth. Wait and see how it all shakes out.

## DIGITAL CASH

Digital cash is an alternative to transmitting credit cards over the Internet. Several companies offer variations on this theme. Acting as on-line banks, they let consumers open accounts, providing Personal Identification Numbers (PINs) for authenticating transactions. Typically, consumers store account numbers in encrypted form on their computers. While some of these companies style themselves as on-line banks, they more often simply act as mediators, keeping customer credit card numbers on file so they can complete credit card transactions with merchants off the Internet.

Participating merchants establish a relationship with a digital cash company, and instead of asking for a credit card number, their computers communicate account information to the merchant's system, automatically handling the funds transfer.

Digital cash systems are safe and effective means for providing secure transactions over the Internet. They have one drawback: Both merchant and consumer must have relationships with the same digital cash provider or the transaction can't happen. In principle, this is no different from the way you use a credit card at a restaurant. In practice, it's very different, because while credit cards have achieved critical mass, digital cash hasn't.

## ENCRYPTED CREDIT CARDS, VERSION 2

Visa and Mastercard have agreed to collaborate in developing a secure approach to transmitting credit card information over the

Internet. While not complete, it seems safe to predict this will become the preferred approach in the not-too-distant future.

# ADVICE

Keyboard sniffers are a theoretical danger as of this writing, and Visa and MasterCard won't wait long to get their system in use. Use the Netscape secure transaction system for the time being, and convert when the Visa/MasterCard system is ready. Consumers already have credit cards, and they're accustomed to providing them to merchants. They'll be much more receptive to credit-card-based approaches than to whole new financial technologies.

# MILLICENT TRANSACTION SYSTEMS

Imagine you're selling information, and you understand no one tidbit you sell has a huge dollar value. You need a system that lets you charge for small sums of money—maybe even sums smaller than a penny.

That's where "millicent" (*milli* being the prefix that means "one one-thousandth of" and *cent* meaning, of course, $0.01) transaction systems come into play.

Millicent systems have a lot in common with digital cash systems. Consumers open an account with a millicent provider and buy their private money—scrip—with their real money. They can then open an account with you and establish a credit balance with scrip from the millicent provider.

As you sell information you meter it, debiting customer accounts as customers buy information from you.

Proponents of millicent systems point to the futility of trying to hack their systems. It's a lot of effort to try to divert such small sums of money. Detractors point to the number of separate intermediaries needed to make these systems work, consumer resistance to a whole new financial system, and, most significant, how hard it will be for consumers to figure out whether they're being charged fairly.

Opinion: don't be the first on your block to jump in, unless a millicent provider offers you a heckuva good deal or unless you're big enough to be a market-maker for this technology. As with digital cash, your transaction system will create a barrier to your customers until these systems reach critical mass.

## CONCLUSION

Many of the availabilities and avoidances described in this chapter didn't exist in the seminal year 1994. By 2004 these may be replaced and replaced again, by the lightning-speed evolution for which the Internet already is becoming famous.

For the marketer, *technique* is less significant than *salesmanship*. Other media have proved this for more than 200 years.

**FIGURE 10–1A**

*Damark makes good use of the "Shopping Cart" metaphor, letting customers order items from each page describing items for sale. Customers simply enter the quantity of each item and the computer keeps track, as it should.*

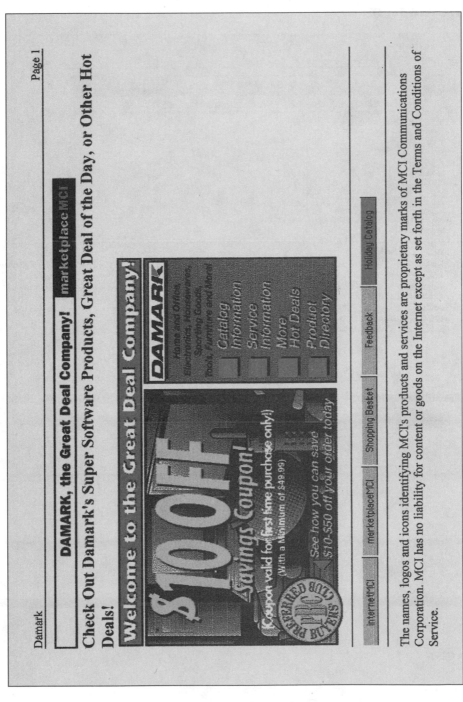

**FIGURE 10–1B**

DAMARK INTERNATIONAL, INC. selection page Page 1

**DAMARK, the Great Deal Company!** marketplaceMCI

**Preferred Buyers' Club Members Save 10%**

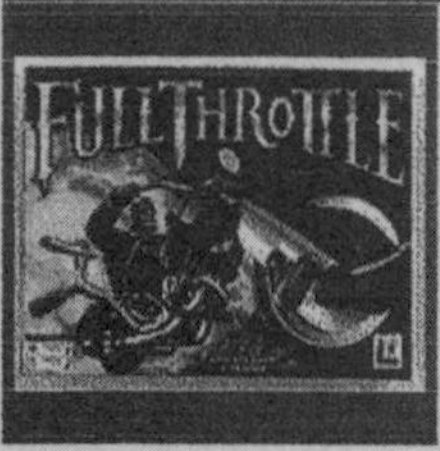


**Full Throttle©**
**455005**
**Manufacturers Suggested Retail: n/a**
**Damark Price: $49.99**
**Kickstart your PC, pull back the throttle and prepare for an action-packed adventure. In Full Throttle, you'll battle against motorcycles, biker gangs and a big, bad world. It features film-animated heavy-metal graphics and a digitized soundtrack featuring a genuine biker band-The Gone Jackals. System requirements: 486DX/33MHz or better, Microsoft(tm) DOS© 5.0 or better, double-speed CD-ROM drive (MPC level 2), 8MB RAM or higher, 1MB of available disk drive space, compatible sound card, 256 color VGA and keyboard required, mouse recommended. CD-ROM version.**
**Shipping & Handling: 5.99**

---

TYPE: PRODUCT

QUANTITY:

Add to basket

Service Department | Storefront | Store Directory

---

---

The names, logos and icons identifying MCI's products and services are proprietary marks of MCI Communications Corporation. MCI has no liability for content or goods on the Internet except as set forth in the Terms and Conditions of Service.

**FIGURE 10–2A**

*Red White and Brew, a beer-of-the-month club, has an excellent Home Page with an atten-tion-grabbing headline, good offers, and clear navigation. Simple-to-use forms make ordering easy, both for personal use and as a gift. Wisely, this marketer offers a toll-free number as an alternative for Web-shy customers.*

# Red, White, & Brew Membership Order Form

## My Information

My Name

Company *(if office delivery requested)*

Street

City

State

Zip

Phone *(home)*

Phone *(office)*

**Yes!** *I would like a Personal Membership that includes 12 bottles of American microbrewed beer and the RW&B newsletter. My total monthly cost will be $15.95 plus tax, shipping and handling. Your membership is ongoing. You may cancel at anytime after 3 months.*

**Yes!** *I would like to give a Gift Membership to:*

If you would like both a Personal and Gift Membership, please check both boxes

Don't forget to fill out the <u>Credit Card</u> information and <u>submit your order</u> at the bottom of this page.

## Recipient Information

**FIGURE 10–2B**

Name of Recipient

Company *(if office delivery)*

Street

City

State

Zip

Phone *(home)*

Phone *(office)*

Length of Gift *(3-month minimum required)*

Each gift membership includes a gift announcement card. Please type a brief message to be included on the card:

Please send the card to me the recipient. Do not send a card.

*Please bill my credit card:*
VISA  Mastercard  American Express

Card #

Expiration Date

By checking this box I authorize Red, White & and Brew to charge my order to my credit card.

*If you prefer to pay in advance by check or money order please call 1-800-670-BREW*

*Void where prohibited by law. Persons under 21 may not participate. Adult signature required upon delivery.*

**FIGURE 10–3A**

*The Great American Beer Club competes directly with Red White and Brew, with no real difference other than writing style. Where Red White and Brew goes for snappy, clever copy, The Great American Beer Club uses more straightforward copy invoking the quality of the beer. The surfer looking for "Beer" has a choice . . . and may choose to sample both.*

# The Great American
# Beer Club

Become a member in the Great American Beer Club and join an expedition to capture the **rarest and freshest** of all natural microbrewed beer. There are no up-front fees or minium membership time required.

**The Perfect Gift
All Year Round!**

Call **1-800-TRY-A-SIP**
to become a member of the Great American Beer Club

**OPEN 24 HOURS A DAY**

**FIGURE 10–3B**

Join an expedition to capture the RAREST & FRESHEST all natural microbrewed beer

Membership Information (USA only) in the <u>Great American Beer Club.</u>

Information on obtaining a <u>Complete Home Brew Kit!</u>

Check out the new <u>Road Map Guide to America's Microbreweries and Brewpubs</u>

---

## <u>ORDER A MEMBERSHIP!</u>

### <u>COOKING WITH BEER: A RECIPE COLLECTION</u>

### <u>E-MAIL THE GREAT AMERICAN BEER CLUB</u>
or call (815) 363-4000

---

### Franchise Opportunity

If any foreign Beer Importer in the countries of Japan, China, Canada, England, Germany, etcetera is interested in importing our rare American Microbrewed beer for their own Beer-of-the-Month-Club Franchise, please contact us.

## FIGURE 10–4A

*From the viewpoint of many site visitors, this is the wrong way to handle on-line ordering. A simple blank order form such as you'd find in a printed catalog forces customers to write down numbers as they browse the site to then re-enter them on the order form. Visitors to the site will all be computer-literate enough to understand how much easier the process could be.*

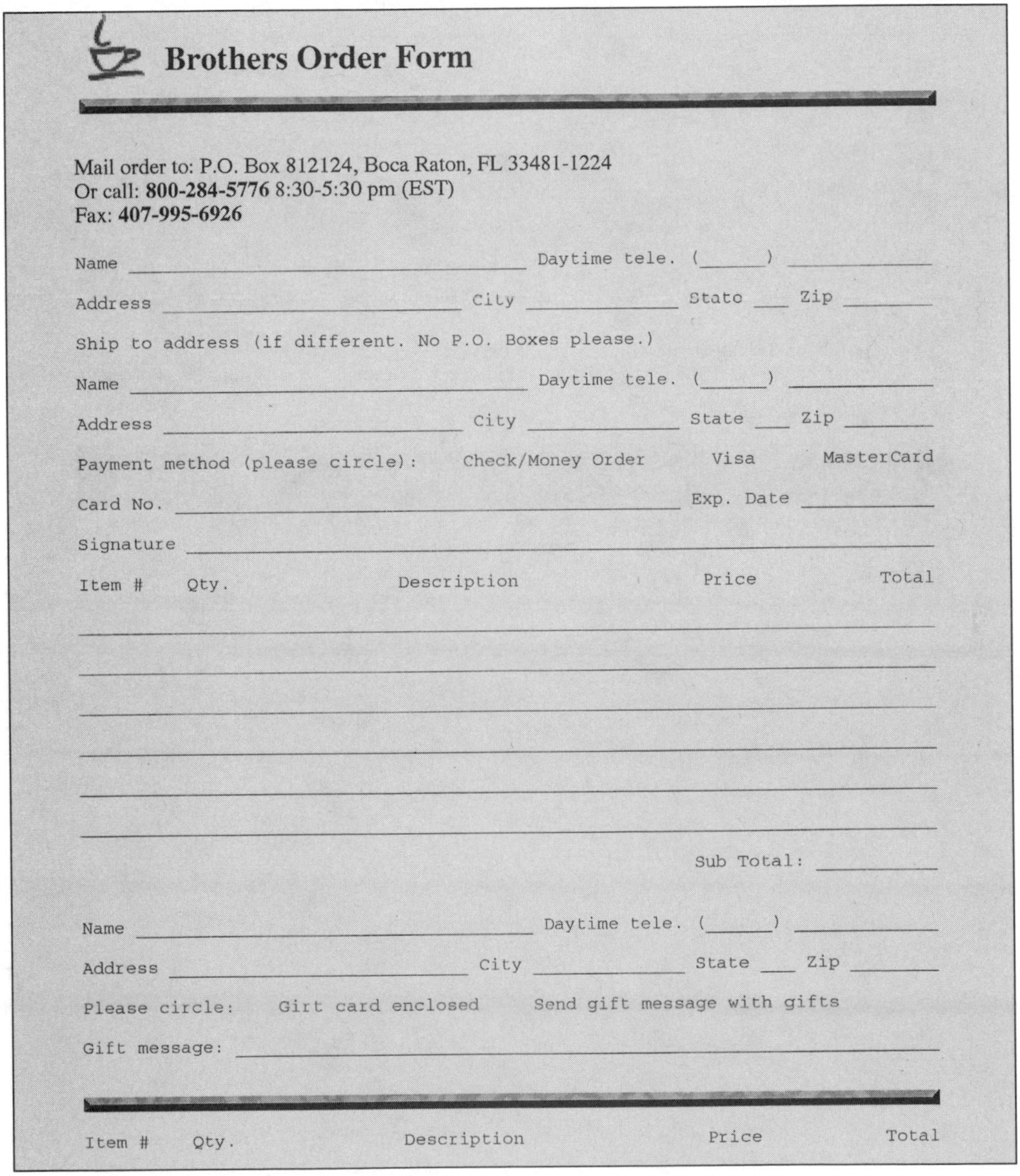

---

### ☕ Brothers Order Form

Mail order to: P.O. Box 812124, Boca Raton, FL 33481-1224
Or call: **800-284-5776** 8:30-5:30 pm (EST)
Fax: **407-995-6926**

Name _____ Daytime tele. (_____) _____

Address _____ City _____ State ___ Zip _____

Ship to address (if different. No P.O. Boxes please.)

Name _____ Daytime tele. (_____) _____

Address _____ City _____ State ___ Zip _____

Payment method (please circle):     Check/Money Order     Visa     MasterCard

Card No. _____ Exp. Date _____

Signature _____

| Item # | Qty. | Description | Price | Total |
|--------|------|-------------|-------|-------|
| | | | | |
| | | | | |
| | | | | |
| | | | | |
| | | | | |
| | | | | |

Sub Total: _____

Name _____ Daytime tele. (_____) _____

Address _____ City _____ State ___ Zip _____

Please circle:   Girt card enclosed     Send gift message with gifts

Gift message: _____

| Item # | Qty. | Description | Price | Total |
|--------|------|-------------|-------|-------|

**FIGURE 10–4B**

_____

_____

_____

                                                        Sub Total: _____

Allow 4-6 weeks for delivery

Purchase Amount      "Snail Mail" Rates      Total merchandise price _____
$0 - $25.00          $4.50
$25.01 - $35.00      $4.95               Colorado State tax 7.3%* _____
$35.01 - $50.00      $5.50
$50.00 +             $5.95            Shipping/handling (see chart) _____
COD                  add $4.50
Next Day             $2.25 per lb.   Each additional address $2.50 _____

                                                        TOTAL: _____

* Sales tax charged on all orders delivered in CO only.
If you need more space or have more "ship to" addresses, please attach an additional sheet of paper.

| HOME PAGE | GIFTS & ACCESSORIES | GOURMET COFFEES | ORDER FORM |

## FIGURE 10–5A

*L.L. Bean has chosen to avoid on-line ordering, providing a toll-free number instead. Going one step farther, the company makes it clear that it could have provided for on-line ordering if it trusted the security of the Internet. Positioning its eschewing of on-line ordering as a customer benefit may be sincere or it may have just been an easy-to-implement alternative to programming an order form and linking it to its order-processing system.*

---

### L.L. Bean Products | Ordering Options | Fit Information

## How to Order from the L.L. Bean Web Site

You will be able to order on-line from the L.L. Bean Web Site as soon as we are satisfied that we can guarantee you a safe and secure environment. Until then, here are three safe, convenient ways to order instead.

> **Please note:**
>
> We will not accept orders via e-mail due to our concerns about the security of your information.

### To Order from the U.S.

☐ By telephone
  Call **1-800-441-5713** anytime.
☐ Using a computer that has word-processing
☐ Using a computer that has no word-processing

### To Order from Other Countries

Please note that if you are ordering from outside the U.S., you must order by telephone for correct local prices, duties and taxes.

### To Order by Telephone from the U.S.

Call **1-800-441-5713**, our special phone line for L.L. Bean Web Site callers. It is toll free and open 24 hours a day.

When you request shipping to another country, product prices and delivery charges will vary. For information, please call **1-800-559-4288**.

### To Order Using a Computer that Has Word-Processing

☐ **Download the order form** (It will be named order.rtf and will run on most computers.) If it does not pop open automatically on your screen, save it to your disk or hard drive as a document and open it the way you normally open documents.

Order Form - Please print in landscape mode (order.rtf, 11K)

☐ **Fill out the order form** Either [a] by typing on your screen, clicking back and forth between the order form and the presentations of the products you are ordering, and then printing it out, or [b] by hand after printing it out. (Please print it sideways in "landscape" mode.)

**FIGURE 10–5B**

☐ **Fax your completed order form** to L.L. Bean at **1-207-552-3080** anytime. Our fax lines are open 24 hours a day, 365 days a year.

☐ **Or mail it to us** at: L.L. Bean, Inc., Freeport, Maine 04033-0001 USA.

☐ **Or use it to order by phone** Many people like to fill out our order form to organize their thoughts before telephoning.

## To Order Using a Computer that Has No Word-Processing

If your computer doesn't word-process or has only the original word-processing software that came with it (such as SimpleText or Write), you can still download and open the order form and lots of other interesting files all over the Internet by using the Adobe Acrobat Reader.

If you have Adobe Acrobat Reader, then:

☐ **Download the Adobe Acrobat version of the order form.** It will pop open automatically on your screen, will be named order.pdf and will run on most computers. If it does not pop open automatically on your screen, save it to your disk or hard drive as an Adobe document and open it the way you normally open Acrobat files.

Order Form - Please print in landscape mode (order.pdf, 9.5K)

☐ **Print and fill out the order form** and mail or fax it to us at your convenience. (Please print it sideways in "landscape" mode.)

If you don't have Adobe Acrobat Reader, click on the name of your computer's operating system below to download a free copy. This will take several minutes, depending on the speed of your modem (different versions vary in file size from 1.5 to 6 megabytes).

☐ Adobe Acrobat Reader 2.1 for Windows(TM)
☐ Adobe Acrobat Reader 2.1 for Macintosh(TM)
☐ Adobe Acrobat Reader 1.0.1 for SGI(TM)
☐ Adobe Acrobat Reader 1.0 for Sun(TM) SPARC(TM)
☐ Adobe Acrobat Reader 1.0 for DOS
☐ Adobe Acrobat Reader 2.1 Beta for Sun SPARC and HP platforms

Once you have downloaded the Acrobat Reader, continue as above, opening the order form and placing your order.

## To Order from Other Countries

To order from outside the U.S., you must order by telephone for correct local prices, duties and taxes.

☐ From Canada, call **1-800-221-4221**, our special phone line for L.L. Bean Web Site callers. It is toll free and open 24 hours a day.

# The Future of the Internet

Never has the future of a medium of communications been murkier. But the Internet "Principles of Power" have emerged and can guide writers and marketers who send commercial messages on this exciting . . . and frustrating . . . new medium.

What does the future hold for Internet marketers?

For quite a while, technology will lead. The new generation of corporate giants such as Netscape, Microsoft, Sun Microsystems and their competitors and allies will race at breakneck speed to create new and exciting ways to present information over the Internet.

As they have done since the mid-1990s, marketers will monitor the activities with their salivary glands in overdrive, watching for the magic moment when enough of their customers can take advantage of the new techniques to warrant inclusion in next week's version of their Web sites.

This chapter won't indulge in the usual flights of fancy regarding what we'll see in the year 2020. In the first place, nobody has the slightest idea, and in the second place it makes no difference in how you plan for your business.

What follows is nearly certain. It's the outgrowth of software now under development, or in some cases already shipping. It's an extrapolation of well-known technical trends. It's a matter of turning ideas on which the technical community has already reached consensus into software products you can buy—and from which you can profit.

# Turning the Web into a Professional Medium

The best news about what is on the technological horizon: we'll have far better ways to achieve the basic levels of professionalism expected (and taken for granted) in other electronic media, that is, the tools to make our sites reliable.

- New Web authoring tools and new versions of HTML will make it far easier to catch dead hypertext links, automatically track changed pages, and manage complex Web sites.

- Server management software will alert Webmasters when sites crash and provide meaningful performance statistics, too. This will help marketers determine when they need to invest in bigger servers and higher-speed links to avoid irritating visitors with unnecessarily slow downloads.

- More sophisticated server software will assure marketers of having a quick response time by making it possible to spread processing load across more than one server and also to schedule updates that automatically take effect—eliminating, for example, holiday offers that hang around like abandoned Christmas trees well into the summer.

# Juicing Up Sites

We also can expect a wide array of improvements both to HTML and the add-ins that make the Web more than just static pages. (WARNING: A little more technobabble coming up.) Within the next few years, and in some cases much sooner (perhaps even by the time you read this), you can expect:

- **More Sophisticated Layout Options:** Right now, the Hypertext Markup Language keeps your layouts pretty simple by not letting you do anything complicated. For better or for worse, though, technologists insist on "improving" things, so expect HTML to become more complicated. The good news here: Soon you won't have to know anything more about HTML than you need to know about PostScript. The not-so-good-news: HTML intrinsically can't support exact layout control. In fact, that's its strength: HTML will continue to be a content-oriented medium with control over rendering separated from document markup.

- **Real Time Audio:** As of this writing, sites provide audio clips by downloading sound files and then playing them. The best that can be said about this technique is that it works. The worst that can be said is that the speed sometimes is pitiful. We're sending voices over telephone lines to people who have to wait minutes to hear them. Real Time Audio will change that: Surfers will click on an icon and start to hear the sound immediately.

- **Real Time Video:** Well, kind of. As with real time audio, we'll gain the ability to watch video over the Internet as soon as we click, instead of waiting for a long and tedious download. The bad news about this: video quality does and will depend on the connection speed, and there are limits to the amount of magic you can get from compression. For most Internet users—those who use 14.4 Kbps or 28.8 Kbps modems—the quality will be equivalent to the jerky, low-quality images associated with videoconfer-encing, not the transparent realism of cable television.

- **Programs:** The now primitive ability to attach computer programs to hypertext links will evolve. Sophisticated, easy-to-use languages will give marketers complete control over their customers' experiences on the Web, customizing the site for each visitor, providing up-to-the-second data, retrieving a crucial piece of information, or tailoring a "closer" based on information in a marketing database.

- **Animation:** Where video involves sending huge amounts of information across the Internet, animation just sends the instructions describing the action—a not-inconsider-able but far less imposing task. If a cartoon-like approach, or maybe animated clip-art, will help you make your point you'll have good tools to help you build your presentation.

- **Virtual Reality:** No, not a goggle-and-glove interface for everyone, cool as that would be. In this context virtual reality refers to the less-ambitious but more useful ability to construct three-dimensional scenes and let the surfer control movement through them. In a parallel use, it will let you construct a computer model of your object and let visitors to your site move around it, rotate it, flip it on its head, change its color and texture, turn its gears, and otherwise manipulate it in space and time.

# More Speed

More than anything else, enhancements to the World Wide Web will depend on more speed. Faster links inside the Internet. Faster computers acting as Web servers. Faster computers on surfer desks to run more sophisticated browsers.

And most important of all, faster links between computers running browsers and the Internet to replace the relatively pokey 28.8 and occasional 33.6 modems that now represent the fastest hookup most consumers can afford.

The good news: the technology exists to make this happen right now.

The bad news: when a technological advance will require a wholesale changeout in an expensive infrastructure (in this case the public telephone system), that advance rarely happens quickly.

Here are the likely ways more speed will happen:

- **Faster Modems:** We're about at the end of the line for traditional analog modems. The proof: when you dial into the Internet with a 28.8 Kbps modem, you usually get a connection somewhere between 14.4 Kbps and 28.8 Kbps. The techniques used by fast modems require noise-free, clean telephone circuits. And no matter how much faster we make the modems themselves, those improvements won't help the phone lines get better. Faster modems just won't do it.

- **ISDN:** an acronym that stands for "Integrated Services Digital Network" (but which most industry insiders will insist really stands for "It Still Dials Numbers"), ISDN replaces the existing analog telephone system with a faster, more reliable digital alternative.

  Residential ISDN service costs more than analog service (how much more depends on which telephone company and which Public Utilities Commission controls the rates in your area). It delivers transmission bandwidth in 64 Kbps chunks—more than twice what you can expect through modems, and without the irritating minute-long delay while your modem dials the telephone and synchronizes with the modem on the other end.

- **Cable Modems:** The cable television companies have threatened to enter the telephone business for a decade. They haven't done so in depth, as of this writing, largely because they aren't used to delivering the quality of service needed to run a telephone system. (Hint: you *always* get a dial tone when you pick up your telephone.)

  Internet connections usually need no more reliability or service quality than cable television, so using the cable network to carry data traffic is a natural extension of the cable business. Cable companies routinely deliver 1 Mbps (that's *million* bit-per-second) and faster service in test markets. The laws of supply, demand, and greed will determine whether this method for delivering high speed Internet access succeeds—not the basic viability of the technology, which has already been proven.

- **ADSL:** Standing for "Asymmetrical Digital Subscriber Line," this technology is the telephone companies' answer to cable modems. It lets telephone companies transmit television-quality signals over existing copper wire into the home. Officially, it's about 6 Mbps. Technically, that translates to "very fast."

  The kicker is the "asymmetrical" part—the signal coming in goes at 6 Mbps. The signal you send back goes much slower—64 Kbps. All in all, consumers probably have less to say to the Internet than it has to say to them, so that's just fine. In other words, a consumer will key in a URL, maybe 25 bytes of data. In response, a 100 kilobyte Web page with an embedded 3 megabyte video clip comes back. ADSL makes a lot of sense.

- **Satellite:** Satellite links are one-way affairs, making them perfect for "cable" television, but inappropriate for an interactive medium like the Internet. One company, Hughes Data Systems, has solved this using an ADSL-like approach. Subscribers send requests for information to Hughes via modem and get Web pages back through the satellite link. This leads to a relatively affordable way to get data transmitted at more than 1 Mbps.

- **Electric Utilities:** It may seem bizarre, but the technology has existed for some time to transmit data back and forth over existing power lines. With deregulation of the power companies driving them into new business models, some power companies may choose to sell data communications bandwidth, to generate more revenue. Probably, this technology can deliver somewhere between 64Kbps and

1Mbps to each home, and needs only an inexpensive gadget (about $40) to convert the incoming power line and make it ready for data transmission.

As the technological universe expands, so will the number of Internet users, far beyond the size of any mailing list other than raw names and addresses, so does the universe of marketers and would-be marketers. So competition keeps pace with market potential, as it usually does.

# Technology Leads, Technological Knowledge Lags

Seniors. Women. Two huge segments, obviously included in the total mix but, except for a handful of target marketers, not exploited.

Does the writer care whether the target is over 55, or female, or both? Does the writer care whether the target is black or Hispanic? The writer had better, just as he/she cares when constructing an ad for Nordic Track or a health-related mailing.

In late 1995, anticipating the fragmentation that can be expected as the potential community of message recipients reaches commercially-exploitable size, America OnLine established "NetNoir," a department aimed exclusively at African-Americans, and "iVillage," dedicated to parenting. In 1996 CompuServe established a separate service aimed at children.

We're used to technology filtering down slowly. If we're marketers, we're used to matching our message to both the medium (implicit) and those who populate the medium (explicit). We're a generation away from taking Internet literacy for granted, just as computer vendors of the early 1970s were a generation away from taking computer literacy for granted.

Those who recognize who's out there *right now* . . . and match their messages to who's out there *right now* . . . may or may not survive. Those who don't certainly won't.

# Women on the Net

Women on-line unquestionably are in a loftier economic bracket than men online. This creates an exciting availability, subject only to (a) the natural growth of this universe and (b) competition. (So what else is new?)

Early thrusts at the women's market recognized the sociological change of the 1990s. *Some* women prefer to be approached *as women*, rather than, as was true half a generation before, as part of a group of genderless targets. The demography of this group skews to upscale, more highly educated, professional, and under 49—ideal marketing grist.

Early marketers include Lang's Women's Web address (http://www.womweb.con) and the lucky owner of the address http://www.women.com—Women's Wire—aimed at the 18-to-40 age group. This site asks women to register before entering, ostensibly to keep others out but probably a marketing ploy to capture names. Opinion: Isolation under the guise of exclusivity may seem to many women to be less exclusive than relegation to a cyberspace ghetto.

Marketing to women on the Internet in many ways parallels advertising in *Working Woman*. Emphasis on ways to save time is more relevant than emphasis on ways to save money. News and products enhancing personal stature supersede entertainment.

This suggests a hybrid word parallel to "infomercial" or "magalog." In this case the word is:

Edutainment.

Like castor oil buried in a chocolate milk shake, the hard sell is a seamless part of apparently useful information.

Can you see the plus and the minus the technique poses? Think for a minute.

Time's up. The minus lies in the ancient equation:

**Sameness = boredom     Overuse = abuse**

What this means, translated into Internet terms, is that the goose eggs are far from golden to begin with; milking the technique over and over again may generate cynical reactions. Or it may not, of course . . . very few people really become tired of entertainment. So as long as the enclosure of educational content doesn't significantly dilute entertainment value, this technique may enjoy great stability.

Even if overuse of this technique does translate to a minus, there's still the plus. It's the explosive growth of Internet attendance. At least through the turn of the century, for each person reliance on edutainment converts downward into a cynic, two or more fresh recruits will be clicking their mice.

A stronger plus might be the historical survival of infomercials and magalogs whose creativity and genuine appeal lift them out of the pack of sameness. After all, reliance on traditional winners isn't automatically a bad course. Only through overuse does such a course become a loser.

# Ripoff Heaven?

Whenever a successful medium of communication surfaces, so do scams and schemes. They're the camp-followers whose overpainted faces attract the troops and damage the image of everybody in town.

As early as November 1995, an official of the Securities and Exchange Commission said, "The boiler-room operations have moved from the telephone to the computer screen." Sure enough, such exotic offerings as emu ranches and eel farms have joined weight-loss programs and wrinkle creams on the Net.

At the moment the risk of a cyberspace scam seems slight, not only because unhappy buyers can "flame" the site but also because the typical surfer isn't representative of the typical easy "mark." More trouble seems to be stemming from online "chat" rooms than from marketing sites.

In these chat rooms, a stock promoter can tout individual stocks, driving the price up artificially. Then the crooks cash out and leave the buyers with losses—a result that may be unethical but may not be illegal. Even if illegal, such procedures aren't part of the Net marketing world.

As the universe of target individuals expands, so too, inevitably, will the number of quasi-marketers, to whom "use" and "abuse" are synonyms, expand. But isn't that true of all history, all media?

# How about Business-to-Business Marketing?

Since the Net is far and away the most niche-driven marketing weapon yet devised, business-to-business is more than logical. In some ways it's easier than business-to-consumer.

That's because many business universes are more vertical, more finite. The more finite the universe, the more possible it becomes to circularize members of that universe, recruiting them to my site.

If I have an offer for advertising agencies, or for purchasing agents, or for bakers, or for dentists, I have both targeted media and mailing lists. Marketers can provoke interest in their sites by suggesting something extraordinary at those sites or by promising a special to come on a specific date.

Easy software can install the marketer's site as a "favorite location," so the surfer—who, once having taken the positive step of entering the address, becomes upgraded to *prospect*—can pop in with a single click.

Prizes can be a huge business-to-business incentive, but the same caveat that applies to other promotions also applies here: Beware of bestowing personal prizes and gifts that might cause intramural criticism, or even dismissal, of the individual.

The easiest and least controversial incentive is a timely discount. Another Networthy incentive is open glorification of an individual, with a new star enjoying a fame-nova each day or each week.

# Dealing with "Reps"

Some of the traditional broadcast station representative firms staked an early claim as "reps" for Websites. Katz Media Group formed an interactive sales division. Petry Media signed to represent sites such as NetNoir and Ingenius. Specialists such as WebRep handled sales for WebPersonals and Marquee. Doubleclick, a spinoff of advertising agency Poppe Tyson, became the sales rep for Excite and giant Netscape. Interactive Media Sales represented Yahoo!, iGuide, Playboy, and Hollywood Online. And so forth.

Most reps settled on CPM—cost-per-thousand—as the basis for billing, with agency commissions from the standard 15 percent to as high as 35 percent. Cost-per-thousand, as we have seen, is a very "iffy" method of gauging Web marketing.

For the advertiser, this has become a mixed blessing. Professional representation brings order from chaos, but it also eliminates the happy-go-lucky deal-making that made the Web attractive to advertisers willing to take a mild gamble.

With one prediction (by consultancy Jupiter Communications) that on-line advertising sales will reach $5 billion by the year 2000, chaos undoubtedly had to give way to order. What will that do to attract or repel Web advertisers? Ask us in the year 2010.

# Newsletters

One of the brightest Internet futures, for both consumer and business marketers, awaits the newsletter.

That's not only because the very nature of a newsletter (properly presented) combines the best of statesmanship and salesmanship; it's also because a marketer can put newsletter teasers onsite, with a more complete version available to those who subscribe—either as online subscribers or for printed or faxed versions.

The newsletter becomes a positive and painless database builder. Many who hesitate to supply name, address, phone, fax, and e-mail for what they fear might be solicitations enter openly, even enthusiastically, into the newsletter arena.

## How Much Technical Knowledge Do You Need?

Old-timers will remember when they could confound newly minted advertising copywriters by asking for a 100-line ad. What's 100 lines? Many a tyro wrote a hundred lines of copy, not knowing the venerable ratio—14 agate lines to the inch.

We have no old-timers on the Net, and terminology is evolving as fast as technology. But we do have a sensible approach, the final two Rules of Internet Advertising.

Final Rule No. 1:

> **Write it the way you want to see and hear it. Include enough instructions so the technicians can produce what you've asked for.**

Final Rule No. 2:

> **Communicating on the Net parallels communicating in any other medium . . . or in person: Terminology is always a less-valuable marketing tool than the ability to generate a desire to buy.**

After all, wouldn't you rather be responsible for a Net profit than a nettled boss or client?

### FIGURE 11–1A

*To keep track of new technologies for the Web and how they're likely to evolve, visit the sites put up by the technological leaders of the Web. Netscape's site shows its own innovations, the innovations of its technology partners, and ideas on how to use the new features it's promoting. It also shows how slowly most of these new features download with 14.4 Kbps modems.*

**ANNOUNCING THE RELEASE OF NETSCAPE NAVIGATOR 2.0 BETA2**
The latest release includes new features. Check out examples of Java, Plug-ins, and LiveScript including WebFX's VRML plug-in. The Netscape Bugs Bounty Program continues with this release. Learn more about Navigator 2.0 and download now !

**NETSCAPE SERVER PERFORMANCE RATED BEST**
Netscape Servers and Netscape Server Application Programming Interface substantially outperform OpenMarket and NCSA servers using APIs and CGIs in WebSTONE benchmark tests of Unix Web servers according to an independent study conducted by Shiloh Consulting and Haynes & Company.

**POWER PACK BUNDLES ADD-ON FOR NAVIGATOR**
Netscape announces Netscape Power Pack 1.0, a suite of add-on applications that extends the capabilities of Netscape Navigator for Windows.

**PRICE CUTS ON NETSCAPE SERVERS**
Netscape announces aggressive price reductions on Commerce and Communications Servers for Unix and Windows NT.

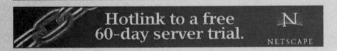

## WELCOME TO NETSCAPE!
**EXPLORING THE NET**
What's New
What's Cool
Net Directory
Net Search**NETSCAPE STORE**
**COMMUNITY**
Netscape User Groups
Internet White Pages**COMPANY& PRODUCTS**
Netscape Products
Netscape Sales
About Netscape
Channel Partners
Development Partners
Business Solutions
**ASSISTANCE**
About the Net
Netscape Support
Creating Net Sites

**FIGURE 11–1B**

NETSCAPE PRODUCTS

## NETSCAPE POWER PACK

 **Netscape Power Pack** is a suite of add-on applications that extends the capabilities of Netscape Navigator for Windows. Combining Netscape SmartMarks, Netscape Chat and multimedia add-on applications from Adobe Systems, Inc., Apple Computer, Inc., and Progressive Networks, Inc., on a CD-ROM, Netscape Power Pack lets customers easily take advantage of five leading add-on applications that enhance the capabilities of Netscape Navigator.

Power Pack enriches the visual and audio experience of the Internet as well, with Adobe Acrobat Reader, Apple QuickTime, and RealAudio Player opening up still and moving images and real-time audio. This CD-ROM-based product's engaging, graphical installation procedure provides clear descriptions of each Netscape Power Pack application, helping users decide which to install.

 **NETSCAPE SMARTMARKS**
Find, monitor, and organize the hottest Net sites.

 **NETSCAPE CHAT**
Communicate with other Net users who share your interests.

 **ADOBE ACROBAT READER**
View electronic PDF documents with WYSIWYG ease.

 **APPLE QUICKTIME**
Play multimedia movies with video and sound.

 **REALAUDIO PLAYER**
Listen to audio over the Net in real time.

**DATA SHEET**
Netscape Power Pack
Netscape Chat
Netscape SmartMarks
Netscape Navigator 2.0
**HOW TO BUY**
Directory of Retailers
Netscape General Store

# Internet Terminology

**Browser** A program which allows users to view and hear information on the World Wide Web.

**Bit** The basic unit of information, which may be either 0 or 1. Data communication is measured in "bits per second" (bps). Typical modems transmit in speeds measured in thousands of bits per second (Kbps).

**Byte** The amount of information (eight bits) needed to describe a single alphabetic character. A "kilobyte" contains 1,000 alphabet characters, a "megabyte" contains a million, and so on.

**FTP** File Transfer Protocol: a function that lets Internet users copy files onto their own computers.

**GIF** Graphic Interchange Format: One of two widely used file formats for graphic images. It makes possible uncomplicated transfer of images between different computer systems. See "JPEG."

**Home Page** The first page anyone sees when visiting a Web site.

**HTML** HyperText Markup Language: The computer language that describes how Web pages should appear and provides the means for describing connections with other pages. By "clicking" on words or phrases for which these connections— "links"—have been established, the user moves to a new page or site described in the highlighted section. Understanding this technique is vital to effective Internet copywriting.

**HTTP** HyperText Transfer Protocol: This is the communications method of moving documents across the World Wide Web.

**Java** A programming language, originally created by Sun Microsystems, that lets page designers attach small programs to hypertext links to animate pages, retrieve information from databases, or otherwise automate an activity.

**JPEG** One of two widely used file formats for graphic images, making it easy to transfer images between different computer systems. See "GIF."

**Mosaic** The original "browser" that set standards for Internet use.

**Search Engine** A free directory to sites on the World Wide Web. Examples: "Web Crawler" and "Yahoo."

**URL** Uniform Resource Locator: A Website address.
Example: *http://www.communicomp.com/response*

**VRML** Virtual Reality Modeling Language: A way to create three-dimensional models, transmit them across the World Wide Web, and let people interact with them through their Browser.

**WWW** World Wide Web: The part of the Internet used for sending graphical, formatted pages back and forth. By convention, this is an integral part of most Web addresses.

# B United Way of Anderson County

Here is a classic example of a straightforward home page with a relatively simple graphic that downloads quickly and contains all the basics on the first screen.

Notice, in particular, the "who, what, where, why, and how" organization of the icons. This certainly isn't the hard-driving, dynamic approach we advocate throughout this book.

But this isn't a hard-driving, dynamic company; it's a charitable organization; and in this Age of Skepticism people want to know more about the charities they support. The pages that immediately follow list members and staff—to attach community identities to the organization. The approach is proper—low-key, straightforward, and unpretentious.

The third page states the United Way's mission—"Somebody to lean on/Your Hometown United Way"—directly and succinctly. The choices that follow—a letter from the president, financial status, a "Look at United Way's programs," a list of local volunteers, and Frequently Asked Questions (FAQs)—should diffuse the wariness from even the most skeptical potential contributor. Only then does a form for giving to the United Way appear.

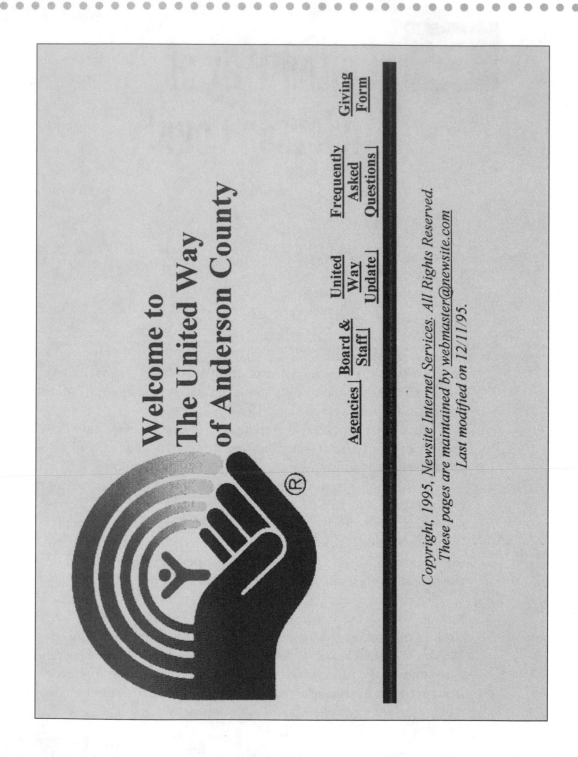

# United Way of Anderson County 1995 Member Agencies

ACCJ-VORP
Ms. Sandra Snyder
Executive Director
P.O. Box 4081
457-5400, 352
Oak Ridge, TN
37831-4081

ADFAC
Ms. Kathy Womac
P.O. Box 5953
Oak Ridge, TN
37831-5953
483-6028

American Red Cross
Mr. Tony Farris
Executive Director
908 Oak Ridge Turnpike
Oak Ridge, TN 37830
483-5641

Anderson County Emergency & Rescue Squad
Mr. James E. Hall
President
450 North Main Street
Clinton, TN 37716
457-7121

Anderson County Health Council
Ms. Jeanie Bertrarn
Coordinator
141 East Broad Street
Clinton, TN 37716
457-4300

Arc of Anderson County
Ms. Billie Fain
Executive Director
P.O. Box 4823
Oak Ridge, TN 37831
457-8080

Big Brothers/Big Sisters

What would you like to do today?

☐ Read a letter from the President of the United Way of Wichita Falls
☐ Look at the financial status of the United Way
☐ Look at the United Way's programs
☐ See who the local colunteers are
☐ Read the Frequently Asked Questions about the United Way

These pages created by David Nelms

# A Letter from the President of the United Way of Wichita Falls

Dear Friends of the United Way,

As the 1994 program year comes to an end, I want to take this opportunity to thank you for your continued support of our United Way and our 26 member agencies. There is no way to adequately recognize all the volunteer time and effort that has gone into our United Way and its affiliated agencies. Over 124,000 persons benefitted from agencies' services, but those serviced would not have been possible without the sacrifices each of you made. On behalf of the United Way Board and our member agencies, I can only say THANK YOU, THANK YOU, THANK YOU.

This past year has not been without its challenges. We had a particularly difficult campaign; and while the final results aren't in, it appears that we will be short of our goal. In fact, we expect to raise less than we did last year. This will impact agency allocations, but the United Way Board will try to minimize that impact every way possible.

I believe the important aspect of the 1994 campaign is that we learn from our experience and grow in the future. Campaign plans are already underway for 1995. Those plans call for new ideas for our campaign and a renewed commitment to the United Way. Our United Way was begun 72 years ago to consolidate fund raising efforts in the community. That continues to be our goal, but we aren't accomplishing it as well as we would like. Ideally, United Way agencies wouldd have to do little or no fund raising on their own. That isn't the case. Ideally, we would be providing funds to more than 26 agencies. That isn't the case either.

I am looking forward to 1995 as a year of renewal. OUr United Way can play a stronger role in our community, but it will require the help and commitment of us all. I would challenge everyone to make this goal for the coming year. The United Way is one of the most efficient and effective ways to raise funds in our community. Please help us improve those efforts in 1995.

**Sincerely, David Wolverton, President**

Click here to go back to the main menu
Click here to go back to the Cyberstation

# Campaign

The most important ingredient in the annual United Way Campaign is the tremendous group of volunteers, who make the campaign possible. That volunteer commitment starts with the Campaign Chairman. This year's chariman was Bob Reed, who devoted countless hours to organizing the campaign, contacting contributors and making presentations to employee groups.

The commitment has it's foundation in the Loaned Executives (LEs), who are "on lean" from their employers or businesses and manage all major employee campaigns. This year, we has 20 LEs, each of whom worked 10 or more companies. They conducted hundreds of rallies at all hours of the day and night. Nearly 60 percent of all funds raised in the campaign is raised through the effort of LEs.

Another vital component is the Company Campaign Coordinator. Coordinators are employees who manage the campaigns in their own companies. They devote time and effort to the success of the campaign. Last but not least, we received tremendous help from United Way agencies, which provided tours, made speeches and generally helped wherever needed. To all of the volunteers, we say thanks.

We are still receiving pledges for the 1994 campaign. To date, the campaign can report $1,605,324, which is 68 ercent of our $1,850,000 goal. Two divisions deserve special mention, because they have exceeded their goal. The Iowa Park Division raised $82,906 (107.7 percent) and the Combined Federal Campaign raised $353,652 (112.6 percent).

**Thank you everyone for your support!!!**

# Budget and Allocations

There are few jobs more difficult than determining how funds are to be used. Each year, about 21 volluntdo just that. These special, concientious people make a concerted effort to learn more about the programs, administrations and financial resources of the agencies and then reccommend funding to the United Way Board of Directors.

The Budget and Allocations committee is divided into three panels of six people. Each panalist is paired with another to form an Advocate Team. The Advocate Teams are responsible for learning about the programs, goals, strengths and weaknesses as well as budgetary needs and financial performance of two to three agencies.

The Committee makes every effort to understand all of the information presented by the agencies as well as utilizing the observations of the Advocate Team to determine funding levels

# Community Services

Generally, our United Way meets area residents' needs through its member agencies. However, our Community Services Division does offer some direct help throughout the year. Our Information andd Referral Service directed hundreds of callers to appropriate agencies, when those individuals needed help.

# Appendix

# AT&T

Here is a home page that tries to have something for everybody. That's certainly implied in "at Home, at Work, around the Globe & on the Net." Aside from possible slow download for this complex page, it may have too many items for the average surfer to focus on.

Someone who already knows what he or she is looking for will welcome the choices. But there are problems with some of the highlighted copy. The uninspired copy in triangles fights with the "AT&T Business Network" and one potential grabber near the lower left corner: "Can you identify today's Microscape?" These, plus the additional four icons along the bottom, might cause as much confusion as help.

This home page is certainly workmanlike . . . but hardly inspired.

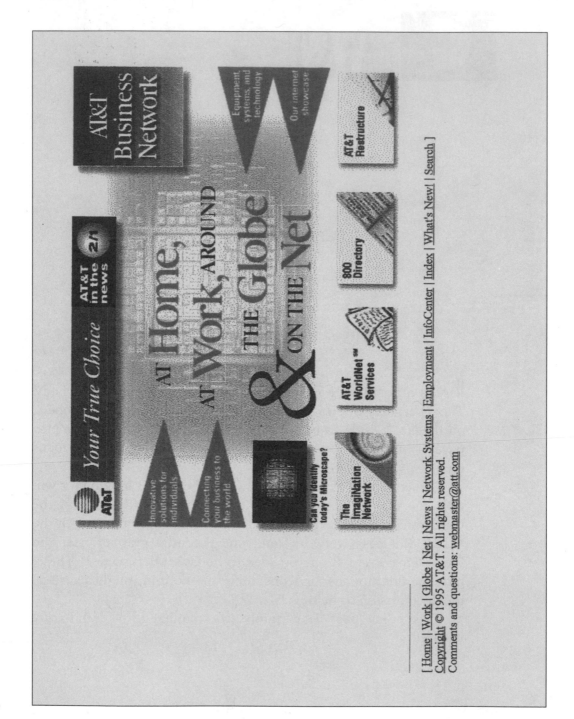

[ Home | Work | Globe | Net | News | Network Systems | Employment | InfoCenter | Index | What's New! | Search ]
Copyright © 1995 AT&T. All rights reserved.
Comments and questions: webmaster@att.com

# AT&T BUSINESS NETWORK

**Finally, an online service that means business.**

There's a wealth of information online that can help your business. Or course, finding the most pertinent pieces and assembling them into information you can actually use can be a full-time job. Unless you've subscribed to AT&T Business Network, the online service exclusively for business.

It's designed to help you do business in new and different ways while saving you valuable time and keeping you better informed. AT&T Business Network helps you cut through the latest news from over 2,500 of the world's most respected information providers, access Internet sites and sort through financial data. It organizes the information your business needs and puts it all at your fingertips. Enroll right now in the new AT&T Business Network, *the* online service for business, and take advantage of special introductory savings.

[ About the AT&T Business Network | Enroll Now | Visit the AT&T Business Site ]

[ AT&T Home Page | At Home | At Work | Building Networks | On the Net | InfoCenter | Search ]

Comments and questions: webmaster@att.com

Hello

You've come to the right place if you're in search of ideas or information about how AT&T can help you get more out of your business. More savings, more innovative ways of using AT&T technology. Or, if you're merely exploring the possibilities of the Web in search of more links for your list, more terrific sites brought to you by AT&T. So welcome why-ever. And before you go, a few words of an explanatory nature.

You'll find all the content grouped into three color-coded areas for easier navigation. Exploration, which we hope you'll do with gusto. Demonstration, which allows us the chance to show versus tell. Transformation, which is our promise to you of the impact AT&T can have on your business. If you need special assistance, just give me a shout. The name's Watson. As in "Mr. Watson, come here, I want you." And I will, just as fast as I can. Just click on the little red square with my likeness.

All right then,

off you go

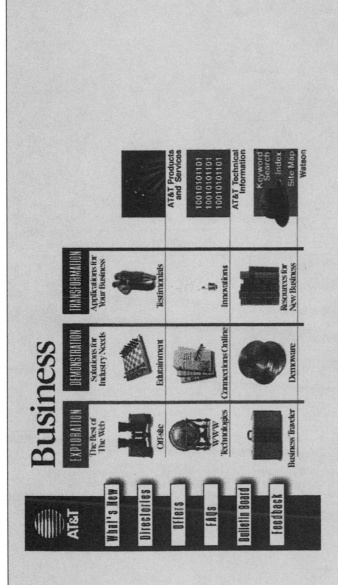

**BROWSE by Category**

Click on the first letter
of a category   A B C D E F G H I J K L M
N O P Q R S T U V W X Y Z

**SEARCH**

To search the AT&T Toll-Free 800 Directory
type in the field below

Select the type of search (default is "And"):

"And" terms          "Or" terms          Exact matches only

After typing and selecting, click here to

Click for <u>help about searching</u> or click to access <u>extended search capabilities</u>.

To bypass downloading graphics, use <u>text-only mode</u>. Give us your <u>feedback</u> about our service.

## Frequently Asked Questions (FAQ)

☐ <u>What is the AT&T Internet Toll-Free 800 Directory?</u>
☐ <u>How Does My Company Obtain a Listing in the AT&T Internet Toll-Free 800 Directory?</u>
☐ <u>What are some Future Enhancements to this Service?</u>
☐ <u>What's New?</u>
☐ <u>Other Commonly Asked Questions</u>

Last update: January 21, 1996.

# Appendix

# D SONY

The SONY home page, while probably difficult to download, is aimed squarely at its proper targets. It tells what SONY does—Music, Electronics, eight categories altogether, including one "Coming This Spring"—in easy-to-read bullets that parallel the highlighted list below. Brief, literal descriptors appear directly below the bullets for those who choose to read, and specific items of interest are described in terse, to-the-point copy beneath hot graphics.

The next page, which picks up the copy below the graphics, follows with an online survey (database!) and a *free* (that old standby motivator) gift. Other features in the list encourage the younger surfer, in particular, to explore SONY's world.

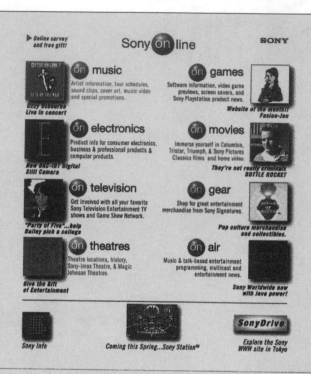

# Welcome to the Sony Online WWW Server!

## Sony Music
Artist information, tour schedules, sound clips, cover art, music video and special promotions.

## Sony Electronics
Product information for consumer electronics, business and professional products & computer products.

## Sony Movies
Immerse yourself into Columbia, TriStar, Triumph & Sony Pictures Classic films, as well as Home Video.

## Sony Television
Get involved with all your favorite Sony Television Entertainment TV shows and Game Show Network.

## Sony Games
Software information, video game previews, screen savers and Sony Playstation product news.

## Sony Theatres
Theatre locations, history, Sony-Imax Theatre, Magic Johnson Theatres.

## Sony Gear
Shop for great entertainment merchandise from Sony Signatures.

## Sony Worldwide
Music and talk-based radio entertainment programming, multicast, and entertainment news.

# What's New!!!

Ozzy Osbourne--Live in concert
New DKC-ID1 Digital Still Camera
They're not really criminals--BOTTLE ROCKET
"Party of Five"...help Bailey pick a college
Website of the Month!! - Fusion-Jan
Give the gift of entertainment
Pop culture merchandise and collectibles
Sony Worldwide--Now with Java Power!

**Online survey and free gift!**

**Sony Information**

**Coming this Spring...Sony Station**

**Explore the Sony WWW Site in Tokyo**

**Send us your feedback!**

Sony online

**Welcome to our special promotion!!! The first 100 people to finish this survey completely will receive a FREE Sony Online T-shirt or a just released Sony Artist CD!**

**Now, all you have to do is fill out the following survey (don't worry, it's not *that* long). We want to know what you want to see at Sony Online, including what you like and don't like about our site. Fill out the survey and maybe you'll be one of the first 100 people to receive a FREE T-shirt or CD!**

Email:

First name:

Last name:

Birthday: MonthDayYear

Gender:  female  male

Address:

City:

State:

Zip:

Country:

Phone:

**How often do you visit Sony Online?**

**How much time do you spend on our site each time you visit Sony Online?**

**What do you like about our site?**

**What do you dislike about our site?**

**What would you change about our site?**

**How did you find out about our site?**

**Which are your three favorite web sites on the net?**
*You can be honest, we won't be offended...*

1.
2.
3.

---

**How often do you log onto the Internet?**

**At what speed?**

**Which online service (if any) do you use?**

America Online          CompuServe

Prodigy                 Delphi

EWorld                  GEnie

MSN

Other

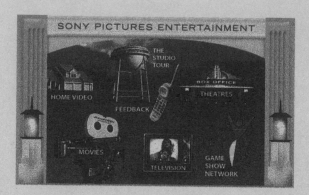

# Welcome to Sony Pictures Entertainment (SPE)!

# Congratulations To All Our Academy Award Nominations!

### "Sense and Sensibility"

**Best Picture** - Lindsay Doran, Producer
**Best Actress** - Emma Thompson
**Best Screenplay based on Material Previously Produced of Published** - Emma Thompson
**Best Achievement in Cinematography** - Michael Coulter
**Best Achievement in Costume Design** - Jenny Beavan, John Bright
**Best Achievement in Music - (Original Dramatic Score)** - Patrick Doyle

### "The American President"

**Best Achievement in Music (Original Music or Comedy Score)** - Marc Shaiman

### Send your Valentine's Day cards online!

Do you want to show that special someone how you feel but don't have time to shop for a card? Well, you're in luck. We've put together a selection of Valentine's Day cards featuring the stars of the most romantic shows on television, "_Days of Our Lives_" and "_The Young and the Restless_." Choose one and send it online to whomever you like. No hassles, no shopping malls, and the best part is... they're free! Also, stop by our romance page for all your Valentine's Day needs.

## Sony Pictures Imageworks Launches CyberPassage

# E GiGi's of Alma

We chose this because it represents the perfect home page for a verticle interest group. Avid cross-stitchers are virtually a closed society. They know what to expect from suppliers—and they get it here. Thirteen uncomplicated, descriptive (for "cross-stitchers"—and that's the market) subjects tell the surfer immediately what he or she needs to know. Three simple icons at the bottom give the direction needed for further information.

The Product Page displays GiGi's offerings in an attractive way. (The copy, reversed out of a dark background, might offend some traditionalists.)

The Order Form gives all the information needed to order and neatly covers both retail and wholesale without irritating either. No one would call this order form anything but utilitarian; but it's consistent with the deliberately unsophisticated image.

As we state elsewhere in this book, the company misses a logical incentive by not giving some sort of discount or indicating a savings for buying off the Net, or buying "right now." The instruction to "Wire payment" is hardly a motivator to the average person, but it is clear and easy to follow—and the way business is done by this group.

# Welcome To GiGi's of Alma
# Cross-Stitch Home Page

*Finished/Framed Cross-Stitched Artwork*

*or*

*Create Your Own With Pattern and Floss*

| About | Products | Order Page |

**Email:** <u>NE-ALM-GJ@NELNK.PSINET.ORG</u>

**Phone:** *(308)928-2211*

**Fax:** *(308)928-2612*

# Serengeti Freedom

This cheetah was photographed by Dr. Leon Long, Professor of Geological Sciences of the University of Texas at Austin. Dr. Long was on vacation at the time he photographed the cheetah in the Serengeti wildlife sanctuary in Tanzania.

The background design was adapted from 100-year-old wallpaper discovered during renovation of a house in Alma, Nebraska.

Home Page    Products    Order Page

# Order Page

All prices are quoted in United States currency, and are subject to change.

## Customer Information:

Name
Email
Address
City
State
Zip
Country
Phone

## Retail Price List

Prices include pattern, embroidery floss, shipping and handling.
Prices **do not** include waste canvas or fabric.

| Item / Item Number | Cost | Quantity |
| --- | --- | --- |
| Colorado Gold (#00195) | $75.60 | (1-19) |
| Majesty (#00994) | $40.40 | (1-19) |
| Platte Sentry (#00294) | $59.65 | (1-19) |
| Serengeti Freedom (#00394) | $82.20 | (1-19) |
| Cagney (#00494) | $43.90 | (1-19) |

## Wholesale Price List

Prices include pattern and embroidery floss. Prices **do not** include shipping charges, waste canvas or fabric. Any combination of designes may be ordered to reach the discount rates for each design. Orders in the United States will be shipped COD; allow 90 days delivery.

Wire payment to:

National Bank of Commerce,
13 & O,
Lincoln, Nebraska 68501, USA
Account #104000045

Correspondent Bank of:

Commercial State Bank,
20 Circle Drive,
Republican City, Nebraska 68971, USA
Account #02 000767

For Credit to:

GiGi's of Alma,
P.O. Box 97,
Alma, Nebraska 68920, USA
Account #160 567

If you have questions regarding payment method, please contact your bank.

Home Page          Products

Ginger Jensen Designer
Email: NE-ALM-GJ@NELNK.PSINET.ORG
Phone: (308)928-2211
Fax: (308)928-2612

# Index

# TITLES OF INTEREST IN
# ADVERTISING, SALES PROMOTION, AND PUBLIC RELATIONS

For further information or a current catalog, write:
NTC Business Books
a division of NTC Publishing Group
4255 West Touhy Avenue
Lincolnwood, Illinois 60646–1975